D1880133

A COMPARATIVE STUDY
OF THE
EARLY TREATISES INTRODUCING
INTO EUROPE
THE HINDU ART OF RECKONING

A COMPARATIVE STUDY
OF THE
EARLY TREATISES INTRODUCING
INTO EUROPE
THE HINDU ART OF RECKONING

SUZAN ROSE BENEDICT

GYAN

Published by

Gyan Publishing House
5, Ansari Road
Daryaganj, New Delhi-110002
Phone: 011-47034999, 9811692060
E-mail: books@gyanbooks.com

Distribution Network
gyanbooks.com
India, USA, Canada, UK, Australia, France

© Publisher

All rights reserved. No part of this work may be reproduced, stored, adapted, or transmitted in any form or by any means, electronic, mechanical, photocopying, micro-filming, recording or otherwise, or translated in any language, without the prior written permission of the copyright owner and the publisher.

ISBN: 978-81-212-9677-9 (PB)
First Published, 1914

2nd Impression 2023

Printed at: Gyan Press, Delhi.

The book is sold subject to the condition that it shall not, by way of trade or otherwise, be lent, resold, hired out, or otherwise circulated without the prior publisher's written consent.

A COMPARATIVE STUDY OF THE EARLY TREATISES INTRODUCING INTO EUROPE THE HINDU ART OF RECKONING
Author: SUZAN ROSE BENEDICT

A COMPARATIVE STUDY

OF THE

EARLY TREATISES INTRODUCING INTO EUROPE

THE HINDU ART OF RECKONING

BY

SUZAN ROSE BENEDICT

April 29, 1914

CONTENTS.

LIST OF TREATISES DESCRIBED.

SECTION I.

Introduction.

In any study of the development of human thought, emphasis is justly laid upon the periods of great discovery, while the centuries in which, through slow evolution, were built the foundations for those discoveries are passed over with a word. Such a period in the development of mathematics we find in the years of transition from the dark ages to the renaissance, when the introduction into Europe of a convenient numerical symbolism furnished one of the most useful tools for the great works of a Descartes or a Newton.

Many manuscripts written during this period are among the treasures of the European libraries, and a bibliography of such works was begun by A. A. Björnbo of Copenhagen, but his early death prevented its completion, and the results of his research are still unpublished.[1] Other historians have found and studied individual treatises, but no careful investigation of the period as a whole has been made, and the best of our histories are unsatisfactory in its treatment.

If however, instead of consulting these works we turn our attention to the monographs which have appeared since the middle of the last century, and to such publications as are found in *Bibliotheca Mathematica, Bullettino di Bibliografia e di Storia delle Scienze Mathematiche e Fisiche, Abhandlungen zur Geschichte der mathematischen Wissenschaften* and *Zeitschrift für Mathematik und Physik*, we find that much has been done to increase the knowledge of this period. Through the efforts of men like Boncompagni, Curtze and Eneström many Latin manuscripts have been discovered and transcribed, and works in the Sanscrit, Arabic and Hebrew have been translated into European languages by such scholars as Colebrooke, Woepcke, Silberberg and Steinschneider; so

[1] Cf. *Über ein bibliographisches Repertorium der handschriftlichen mathematischen Literatur des Mittelalters. Bibl. Math.* IV$_3$, pp. 326–333.

that with the increasing quantity of material available, there will come in the near future a much more complete knowledge of the mathematics of the middle ages.

It has been with the hope of making a contribution to such knowledge that the research, the results of which are embodied in this paper, has been carried on. As a first step it seemed advisable to find the arithmetics of this period which have been published, and to make a bibliography which may perhaps save valuable time for some later study. Accordingly, a systematic search has been made, and all the treatises found, unless dealing exclusively with abacus reckoning, have been noted. There is included in this bibliography, where it has been possible to find such information, the name and date of the treatise, a few words concerning the author, the library where the manuscript may be found and the journal or monograph in which it is published. There is added to this, a brief account of the contents, the approximate length, and in the case of the Latin works, the words of the beginning and end.

These arithmetics have been read throughout, but since many of them are long and treat of a variety of subjects, it has been found necessary to limit the scope of this paper to a discussion of the fundamental operations upon integers. Accordingly, the various methods of performing the operations are described, and a comparison of them is made in order to ascertain to what extent the Latin works were derived from Arabic sources and which of the algorisms were most influential in determining the character of later treatises.

The library of the University of Michigan is exceptionally well fitted for research of this nature, for its files of journals are unusually complete and many rare books are in its possession. For an opportunity to study the *Algorismus demonstratus* of Gernardus and the *Algorismus de integris* of Beldamandi, my thanks are due to Mr. G. A. Plimpton of New York, whose generosity is well known to students of the history of mathematics. The 1534 edition of Peurbach's arithmetic was loaned from the library of Professor L. C. Karpinski, who has directed this investigation, and constantly placed at my disposal his wide knowledge of the works of the period in question. It is with a full appreciation of my indebtedness to him that I acknowledge that without his advice and encouragement my work could not have been completed.

SECTION II.

Bibliography of Sources.

I. GANITAD'HYAYA OF BRAHMAGUPTA.

The 12th chapter of the astronomical work *Brahma-sidd'hánta* translated into English and published, together with selections from a commentary by Chaturveda, by Henry Thomas Colebrooke (*Algebra with arithmetic and mensuration from the Sanscrit of Brahmagupta and Bhaskara, London, 1817, pp. 277-378*).[1]

This is a work on arithmetic, and is divided into ten sections as follows:

1. Operations with fractions, proportion and barter.
2. Mixture.
3. Progressions.
4. Plane figures.
5–8. Solid figures.
9. Shadows.
10. Supplement, treating of multiplication and division.

Brahmagupta was an astronomer who lived in Ujjain in western India, in the 7th century A. D.

II. ALGORITMI DE NUMERO INDORUM.

A unique algorism of the 12th century, probably the earliest translation into Latin of the arithmetic of Al-Khowarizmi. The Arabic original is lost, and the translator is unknown. The manuscript is in the library of the University of Cambridge, where it was discovered by Prince Baldassare Boncompagni by whom it was transcribed and printed. (*Trattati d'Arithmetica I, Rome 1857.*)[2]

This work contains about 5000 words. It treats of the fundamental operations with integers, using in most cases

[1] The copy read is in the library of the University of Michigan.
[2] The copy read is in the library of the Department of Mathematics of Smith College.

the Roman numerals, and gives also a short discussion of fractions. It begins as follows:

> *Dixit algoritmi: laudes deo rectori nostro atque defensori dicamus dignas, que et debitum ei reddant, et augendo multiplicent laudem.*

and ends abruptly with the unfinished sentence.

> *Post hec scribes in alia parte .VIII. et sub eis tres, et sub tribus .XI. sicque constitues .VIII. . . .*

Mohammed ibn Musa Al-Khowarizmi was an Arabic mathematician and astronomer who lived in Bagdad during the reign of the Caliph Al-Mamun, in the first half of the 9th century A. D.

III. GANITA-SARA-SANGRAHA OF MAHAVIRACARYA.

A Hindu work on arithmetic written about 850 A. D. It was translated into English by M. Rangācarya, and published by the government of Madras. (*The Ganita-sára-sangraha of Mahāviracāryā, Madras 1912.*)[1] The published work contains, besides the translation and notes by the translator, the Sanscrit text and an historical introduction by Professor D. E. Smith of Columbia University. The subject matter is divided into nine chapters as follows:

1. Terminology.
2. Arithmetical operations.
3. Fractions.
4. Miscellaneous problems on fractions.
5. Rule of three.
6. Problems.
7. Measurement of areas.
8. Excavations.
9. Shadows.

This arithmetic is not mentioned by Bháskara, and may have been unknown to him, possibly because the author was of the Jaina religion, or because of the distance between the two schools. It was widely known and used in Southern India.

[1] The copy read is in the library of the University of Michigan.

IV. THE ARITHMETIC OF KUSCHYAR IBN LABBAN.

An Arabic arithmetic written about the middle of the 10th century, a Hebrew translation of which made in the 15th century is in the Bodleian Library. A short analysis of the contents is given by Steinschneider in his article on Abraham ben Esra.[1]

The work is divided into twelve chapters dealing with the operations of arithmetic.

V. TRISATIKA OF SRIDHARACARYA.

A Hindu arithmetic written about 1020 A. D. Several manuscripts are extant in India, and a Sanscrit text was published in 1899. This has been translated into English by Professor N. Ramanujacharya of Madras, and was published with introduction and notes by G. R. Kaye.[2] In the same article there is printed a fac-simile of one page of the Benares manuscript. The translation, which contains about 2500 words, discusses the operations with integers and fractions and a variety of other subjects such as interest, partnership and mensuration.

In the opening sentence Śrīdhara states that this is a part of a larger work written by himself, and it is Kaye's opinion that Bháskara's *Lilavati* is based upon it.

VI. THE ARITHMETIC OF AL-NASAWI.

An Arabic arithmetic whose title is *The Satisfactory One.* It was the revision of a similar work written in Persian, and as is stated in the introduction, was composed after a careful examination of all existing works on the subject.

The manuscript is in Leyden. The introduction has been translated into French, and an analysis of the contents made by Woepcke.[3] The work is divided into four books as follows:

[1] *Abhandl. zur Gesch. der Math. III. p. 105.*
[2] *Bibl. Math. XIII₃. pp. 203–217.*
[3] *Journal Asiatique, 16, pp. 491–500.*

1. Operations with integers.
2. Operations with fractions.
3. Integers and fractions.
4. Degrees and minutes.

Al-Nasawi was a mathematician of the court of the Caliph Abdulla, who ruled 997–1029 A. D.

VII. THE ARITHMETIC OF AVICENNA.

An Arabic arithmetic of the 11th century, a part of which was translated into French by J. J. Marcel from a manuscript in his own library.[1] The title of the work is *A letter which opens the doors of the academy by explaining the root of calculation in arithmetic.* The fragment published treats only of the check by nines in the operations with integers, the remainder after division by nine being called the *root*.[2]

Abou Ali el-Hosein ibn-Abdallah ibn-Sina was a physician, philosopher and mathematician, and one of the most celebrated of the Arabic scholars of the 11th century. From his own biography we have evidence that he learned the methods of Hindu calculation from a merchant in Bokhara.[3]

VIII. AL KAFI FIL HISAB OF AL-KARKHI.

An Arabic arithmetic translated into German by Hochheim. (*Kâfî fîl Hisâb des Abu Bekr Alhusein Alkarkhi. Halle 1878–1879.*)[4] The manuscript from which this translation is made is in the library of the Ducal Palace at Gotha, and the frequent mistakes and omissions show it to be a copy rather than the original treatise. The complete work contains about 30000 words in the translation. It treats of multiplication and division of integers and fractions (addition of fractions is treated in connection with multiplication), applications to mercantile life, proportion, extraction of roots, mensuration and algebra. The Hindu numerals are not

[1] The translation is given in the article on *Arithmetic* in Montferrier's *Dictionnaire des sciences mathématiques*, to be found in the Peabody library in Boston.

[2] In his article *Propagation des chiffres Indiens*, in *Journal Asiatique* I_6, pp. 501–507, Woepcke refers to a *Speculative Arithmetic* by Avicenna, to be found in the Library of Leyden, in which is emphasized the check by nines in the case of squares and cubes.

[3] Cf. Carra de Vaux, *Avicenna*, p. 132.

[4] The copy read is in the library of the University of Michigan.

used in the text, and long processes are explained wholly by the use of words.

Al-Karkhi was an Arabic scholar in Bagdad during the first half of the 11th century. Both this work and his treatise on algebra, called *Al Fakri*, were written probably between 1010 and 1016 A. D.

IX. THE ARITHMETIC OF AL-HASSAR.

An Arabic arithmetic of the 12th century, a manuscript of which copied in 1432 is in the Library of the Ducal Palace at Gotha. A description of the contents was published by Suter.[1] The work is divided into seven chapters including operations with integers, operations with fractions, extraction of roots and approximations.

X. LILAVATI OF BHASKARA.

The introduction to an astronomical work, the *Sidd'hanta-sirómani*, which was completed not later than 1150 A. D. The *Lílávatí* was translated into English by Colebrooke (*Algebra with arithmetic and mensuration from the Sanscrit of Brahmagupta and Bhaskara, London 1817, pp. 1–127*).[2] This work is divided into thirteen chapters, these being subdivided. Besides the operations of arithmetic, it treats of many other subjects such as proportion, progression, measurement of plane surfaces and of mounds of grain, and the shadow of a gnomon.

Bhaskara was an astronomer and mathematician of Ujjain, in western India, who lived in the first half of the 12th century.

XI. JOANNIS HISPALENSIS LIBER ALGORISMI DE PRATICA ARISMETRICE.[3]

A 12th century algorism, the manuscript of which is in the National Library in Paris. It was transcribed and published by Boncompagni (*Trattati d'Arithmetica II, Rome, 1857*).[4]

[1] *Das Rechenbuch des Abu Zakaraja el-Hassar. Bibl. Math.* 2_3, *pp. 12–40.*

[2] The copy read is in the library of the University of Michigan.

[3] Referred to hereafter as *Liber algorismi.*

[4] The copy read is in the library of the Department of Mathematics of Smith College.

At least three other manuscripts containing parts of the same work are known, one of which concludes with the words *Explicit liber algorismorum et omnium fraccionum in numeris translatus ex arabico a magistro G. cremonensi.*[1] This work contains about 20000 words, and begins with a treatise on algorism evidently taken from the arithmetic of Al-Khowarizmi or one of its translations. It contains also a series of excerpts unrelated to one another or to the algorism.[2] The treatise begins as follows

> *Incipit prologus in libro alghoarismi de pratica arismetrice. Qui editus est a magistro Iohanne yspalensi.*
>
> *Quiquis in quatuor matheseos disciplinis efficatius uult proficere, numerorum rationes primum studeat apprehendere*

and ends with the words

> *Quiquid exierit de diuisionibus, erunt denominata a fractionibus majoribus.*

followed by a magic square.

John of Spain, also known as John of Luna, was a Jewish scholar converted to Christianity, who under Raimond, Archbishop of Toledo (1130–1150) became a translator of Arabic works.

Girard of Cremona (1114–1187) travelled in Spain, studied in Toledo and translated many philosophical and scientific works from the Arabic.

XII. A TWELFTH CENTURY ALGORISM.

The introduction to a treatise on astronomy, the authorship of which is unknown, though investigations by Paul Tannery point to Adelard of Bath. Several manuscripts are known,[3] and one which is in the Royal Library at Munich, has been transcribed by Max Curtze[4] who states that it was copied by Frater Sigsboto, a brother of the Cloister Prüfning at Regensburg under the Abbot Eberhard (1163–1168).

The algorism contains about 3000 words and treats of the fundamental operations with integers and fractions. It begins

[1] Cf. Wappler. *Abhandl. zur Gesch. der Math. V, p. 159.*

[2] Cf Friedlein, *Die Zahlzeichen und das elementare Rechen der Griechen und Römer und des christlichen Abendlandes, p. 155.*

[3] Cf. Bibl. Math. V₃, p. 312, also Zeitschr. für Math. und Phys. XXXIV, Hist. Abt. p. 129–146.

[4] *Abhandl. zur Gesch. der Math. VIII, pp. 1–27.*

Quoniam de quarta introducendis matheseos nos fari disciplinarium praesens tempus ammonuit.

and ends with the words

quia ista inter se illa producunt, quando radices ad sua integra reducantur, ut possunt. Hactenus de radicibus.

Adelard of Bath was one of the earliest European students of Arabic science and philosophy. He was born in England, probably before 1100, studied in France, travelled extensively in the East and returned to Bath before 1130. Numerous translations as well as several independent treatises are ascribed to him. Among the translations are the astronomical tables of Al-Khowarizmi.

XIII. THE ARITHMETIC OF RAOUL DE LAON.

An arithmetic found in Paris, which has been transcribed and published, with an introduction by Nagl.[1] Though the writer was probably familiar with the methods of the algorists, the work is almost wholly an explanation of the abacus reckoning, and is included in this bibliography only because his method of multiplication resembles somewhat that of the algorists. The treatise contains about 15000 words. It begins

"Incipit liber Radulfi laudunsis de abaco."

and ends

"que magis proximat octaue decime maius semitonium minus."

Raoul de Laon, a brother of the celebrated Anselm de Laon, lived and taught in Paris in the first half of the 12th century.

XIV. SEFER HA-MISPAR OF RABBI BEN ESRA.

A Hebrew arithmetic translated into German and printed with the Hebrew text, and comments on the same by Moritz Silberberg (*Das Buch der Zahl des R. Abraham ibn Esra, Frankfort, a. M.*, 1895).[2] In the translation the work has about 20000 words and treats of the fundamental operations with integers and fractions.

[1] *Der arithmetische Tractat des Rudolph von Laon, Abhandl. zur Gesch. der Math.* V, p. 85–133.

[2] The copy read is in the library of the University of Michigan.

Rabbi Abraham ben Esra, one of the most learned Jewish scholars of Spain, travelled extensively and died in Rome in 1167. His writings are on many subjects including grammar, philosophy and astronomy.

XV. OPUS NUMERORUM AND DEMONSTRATIO JORDANI.

Works ascribed to Jordanus Nemorarius, the latter probably a revision of the first. A description and comparison of the two treatises has been published by Eneström.[1] The date of these works is probably early in the 13th century. The author is evidently attempting to justify by a course of deductive reasoning the methods of arithmetical reckoning, a knowledge of which is presupposed.

Jordanus Nemorarius who lived in the first half of the 13th century is probably identical with Jordanus Saxo, a General of the order of Dominicans.

XVI. LIBER ABACI OF LEONARD OF PISA.

The great work by Leonard of Pisa, written in 1202 to introduce the Hindu Arabic art of reckoning. It was revised in 1228, and dedicated to Michael Scott, the court astrologer to Emperor Frederick II; and the revised text was transcribed and published by Boncampagni (*Liber abbaci di Leonardo Pisano, Rome* 1857).[2] The *Liber abaci* is a large book of 459 pages. It is divided into fifteen chapters, as follows:

1–7. Numeration and operations upon integers and fractions.
8–11. Applications.
12. Series and proportion.
13. Rule of false position.
14. Square and cube root.
15. Geometry and algebra.

The work begins as follows

Incipit liber Abaci Compositus a leonardo filio Bonacij Pisano. In Anno M°cc°ij.° Scripsistis mihi domine mi magister Michael Scotte,

[1] *Uber die Demonstratio Jordani de algorismo, Bibl. Math.* VII₃, pp. 24–37, and *Uber eine dem Jordanus Nemorarius zugeschriebene kurze Algorismusschrift, Bibl. Math.* VIII₃, pp. 135–153.

[2] The copy read is in the library of the Department of Mathematics of Smith College.

summe philosophe, ut librum de numero, quem dudum composui, uobis transcriberem.

Leonard of Pisa, also known as Fibonacci, was, as his name indicates, a native of Pisa. His father having been sent by the government to Bugia in northern Africa, Leonard spent his youth in that city, which was an important center for merchants and scholars and there learned the use of Hindu numerals. He travelled in Egypt, Syria and Greece, and returned to Italy where he wrote the *Liber abaci* containing all that he had learned of arithmetic.

XVII. CARMEN DE ALGORISMO OF ALEXANDER DE VILLA DEI.

A Latin algorism written in verse, consisting of 284 lines. It was published by James Orchard Halliwell from a manuscript in the British Museum (*Rara Mathematica, London 1839*).[1] The large number of manuscript copies to be found in the libraries of Europe prove that it was widely known and used, but in spite of its importance Cantor describes it in one short paragraph, and it is rarely mentioned in other works on the history of mathematics.

The algorism treats of the fundamental operations with integers the explanations being wholly rhetorical. It begins as follows

Haec algorismus ars praesens dicitur, in qua
Talibus Indorum fruimur bis quinque figuris.

and ends.

Si tres vel duo series sint, pone sub una,
A dextris digitum servando prius documentum.

Alexander de Villa Dei was a native of Villedieu in Normandy who taught and wrote in Paris. He died in 1240. Among his works, all of which are written in verse, is a Latin Grammar which was widely used.

XVIII. ALGORISMUS VULGARIS OF JOHN OF SACROBOSCO.

A Latin arithmetic setting forth the new methods of reckoning, which was the most widespread treatise on the

[1] The copy read is in the library of the University of Michigan.

subject during the period 1250–1550. The first edition, printed in Strassburg in 1488, was followed by several others.[1] It appeared in Halliwell's *Rara Mathematica* under the title *Tractatus de arte numerandi*, and a Paris edition of 1510 is called *Oposculum de praxi numerorum quod Algorism vocant.* The best edition is that by Curtze from a manuscript in Munich (*Petri Philomeni de Dacia in algorismum vulgarem Johannis de Sacrobosco commentarius, una cum algorismo ipso edidit, Copenhagen, 1897.*)[2]

The work contains about 4000 words, and treats of the fundamental operations with integers. It begins

> *Omnia, quae a primaeva rerum origine processerunt, ratione numerorum formata sunt,*

and ends

> *Et haec de radicum extractione dicta sufficiant tam in numeris quadratis quam in cubicis. Explicit.*

> John of Sacrobosco was born at Halifax, studied at Oxford and taught in Paris in the first half of the 13th century.

XIX. SALEM CODEX.

A Latin manuscript formerly belonging to the Salem Cloister on Lake Constance and now in the University Library at Heidelberg. It was transcribed by Moritz Cantor.[3]

The treatise is anonymous and undated, but because of textual evidence, such as the forms of the numerals and the abbreviations of words, Cantor places the date at 1200 or earlier. A comparison with other works of the period seems to show, however, that it was written somewhat later, probably in the 13th century.

[1] Curtze mentions more than 60 manuscripts, and says that there must be many more in the libraries of Europe. There are two in America, one in the Plimpton collection and one in the library of Columbia University. Cf. L. C. Karpinski, *Am. Math. Mo. XVII, p. 111*, also D. E. Smith, *Rara Arithmetica*, pp. 31–33.

[2] My study of Sacrobosco's work was from this edition. It is in the library of the Department of Mathematics of Smith College.

[3] *Zeitschr. für Math. und Phys.* X, pp. 1–16.

The treatise contains about 4000 words and explains the fundamental operations with integers attaching a mystic meaning to each. It begins;

"*Omnis sapientia sive scientia a domino Deo; sicut scriptum est:*"

and ends

" . . . *ab hoc saeculo nequam et perducere in vitam aeternam, qui vivat et regnat.*

XX. TALKHYS OF IBN AL-BANNA.

An Arabic arithmetic, a manuscript of which is in the Bodleian Library. This was translated into French by Aristide Marre.[1] The work is divided into two parts. The first of these parts, with the heading *Known numbers* treats of arithmetic and contains about 6000 words. It is broken up into three sections in which are considered (1) fundamental operations with integers, (2) fractions (3), roots. The second part, containing about 900 words, deals with *algebr* and *almokabalah.*

Al-Banna was a teacher of mathematics in Morocco in the first half of the 13th century. He was known as one of the most learned men of his times.

XXI. PROLOGUS N. OCREATUS IN HELCEPH AD ADELARDUM BATENSEM MAGISTRUM SUUM.[2]

A Latin work, a manuscript of which in the National Library in Paris was transcribed by Ch. Henry.[3] In the earlier editions of his history Cantor assumes that Ocreatus was a pupil of Adelard of Bath, but in the latest edition suggests an unknown Adelard of Bayeaux.[4] The probable dedication to Adelard of Bath, as well as the use of Roman numerals throughout the work, and of τ for the zero, point to a date not later than the last half of the 12th century.[5]

[1] *Atti dell' accad. Pont. de nuovi Lincei,* XVII, p. 289–319.

[2] Referred to hereafter as *Ocreatus.*

[3] *Abhandl. zur Gesch. der Math.* III, p. 131–139.

[4] ed. 1907, vol. I, p 906. Haskins, *Eng. Hist. Rev.* XXVI, p. 497, note, asserts that this suggestion is due to an incorrect reading of the text.

[5] Cf. *Bibl. Math.* VIII$_3$, p. 188.

The arithmetic contains about 1800 words, and after a short discussion of numbers treats of multiplication and division. It begins as follows:

> "*Virtus amicitiae inter eos qui ejus habitu inficiuntur hanc legem constituit ut alterutro praecipiente alter parere non pigritetur.*"

XXII. ALGORITHMUS DEMONSTRATUS.

An algorism copied by Regiomontanus and edited by Joannes Schonerus (*Norimbergae apud Io. Petrium Anno MDXXXIIII*).[1] It was at different times attributed to Regiomontanus who was simply a transcriber and to Jordanus Nemorarius,[2] but recent investigations have shown that the author was a certain unknown Magister Gernardus.[3] Several manuscripts of the work are known, of various dates ranging from the 13th to the 16th centuries, that from which the Schonerus edition was taken being found in Vienna.

Under the title *Der "Algorismus de integris" des Meisters Gernardus*[4] Eneström has published a transcription of this treatise from a manuscript in the Vatican, with notes comparing it with *Demonstratio Jordani* and *Opus Numerorum.* The resemblances are striking, both as to the character and the arrangement of the work, and the technical words used, and it seems possible that the work of Gernardus was based upon those of Jordanus Nemorarius.

The algorism contains about 20000 words and is divided into two parts, the first of which treats of operations with integers, and the second with fractions. Each part is subdivided into short propositions, letters being used in the demonstrations, in which are frequent references to the *Elements* of Euclid. The work begins

> *Digitus est omnis numerus minor decem* .

and ends

> *Haec sunt quae de minutiis scienda, ideo colligenda putaui*
> *Algorithmi demonstrati finis.*

[1] The 1534 edition from the library of Mr. G. A. Plimpton was used in the preparation of this paper.

[2] In the last edition of Cantor's history it is attributed to Jordanus.

[3] Cf. Duhem, *Bibl. Math. VI₃, p. 9–15.*

[4] *Bibl. Math. XIII₃, p. 289–332.*

XXIII. A FRENCH ALGORISM.

An ancient French work on algorism. It was transcribed by Ch. Henry from an anonymous 13th century manuscript in the Bibliothéque St. Geneviève[1] and by Victor Mortet, who used also for his transcription a manuscript in the Bibliothéque Nationale.[2] The work, which contains about 800 words, is evidently a translation of parts of the *Carmen de Algorismo.*

XXIV. A THIRTEENTH CENTURY ALGORISM.

An anonymous work. The manuscript, formerly in the possession of Leibnitz and now in the Royal Library in Hanover, was transcribed by C. I. Gerhardt (*Programm, Salzwedel*, 1853).[3]

The treatise contains about 3000 words and explains the fundamental operations with integers. It begins

Quis titulus huius artis. Quid in ea doceatur.

and ends

. . . *sic tamen ut minor auferri non possit a majore secundum artem minor cyfram proponens et negocium.*

XXV. COMMENTUM MAGISTRI PETRI PHILOMENI DE DACIA.[4]

A commentary of about 18000 words on the *Algorismus vulgaris* of Sacrobosco, transcribed by Max Curtze and printed with the algorism (*Petri de Dacia in algorismum vulgarem Johannis de Sacrobosco commentarius, Copenhagen 1897*).[5] The manuscript used is in the Royal Library in Munich. Four other copies are mentioned by Curtze.[6] In this work are found not only careful and scholarly explanations of the text of Sacrobosco, and numerous illustrative examples,

[1] *Bullettino di bibl. e di storia del. scienze math. e fisiche XV, p. 53.*

[2] *Bibl. Math.* IX_2, p. 55–64.

[3] The copy read is in the library of L. C. Karpinski.

[4] Referred to hereafter as *Petrus de Dacia.*

[5] The copy read is in the library of the Department of Mathematics of Smith College.

[6] *Introduction, p. IV, note.*

but also additions to the algorism especially in the matter of proofs and the subject of series and progression. The commentary was written in 1291 and the author may have been that Petrus de Dacia mentioned as Rector of the University of Paris in 1326.[1]

XXVI. SEFER MAASSEI CHOSCHEB OF LEWI BEN GERSON.

A Hebrew arithmetic written in 1321, translated into German by Gerson Lange (*Sefer Maassei Choscheb. Die Praxis des Rechners. Ein hebräisch arithmetisches Werk des Levi ben Gerschon aus dem Jahre 1321. Frankfort a. M. 1909*).[2] A description of the same work appears in a dissertation by Joseph Carlebach (*Lewi ben Gerson als Mathematiker, Inaugural Dissertation, Heidelberg*).[3] Several manuscripts are known, some of them copied as late as the 16th century.

The first part of the work is concerned with algebra, based on the arithmetic of Euclid, and the second part contains a description of number and of the operations upon integers and sexagesimal fractions.

Lewi ben Gerson was a Jewish Rabbi who lived in the first half of the 14th century. He was known in the middle ages as Leo Hebraeus and was celebrated as an astronomer and a mathematician.

XXVII. AN ICELANDIC ALGORISM.

A translation of the *Carmen de algorismo*, written about 1325–1330, by a secretary of the celebrated Icelander, Haukr Erlendsson. A manuscript in the University Library, Copenhagen, was transcribed and published with notes, by Prof. Finnur Jónsson. (*Hâuksbók, Copenhagen 1892–1896, pp. 417–424.*)[4]

[1] Cf. L. C. Karpinski, *Am. Math. Mo. XVII, p. 111.*
[2] The copy read is in the library of the Department of Mathematics of Smith College.
[3] This is in the library of L. C. Karpinski.
[4] The copy used is in the library of Cornell University.

This algorism contains about 2700 words, and though in a few places it differs from that version of the *Carmen* published by Halliwell, it is without doubt a translation of the same work.

XXVIII. THE ARITHMETIC OF PLANUDES.

A Greek arithmetic, the manuscript of which is in the National Library in Paris. It was published in the Greek by C. I. Gerhardt (1865), and translated into German by Hermann Wäschke (*Das Rechenbuch des Maximus Planudes, Halle 1878*).[1] In the German the work contains about 15000 words. It discusses the fundamental operations with integers and astronomical fractions.

Maximus Planudes was a Greek monk who lived in the first half of the 14th century. He was sent as ambassador to Venice in 1337, and lived much of his life in Constantinople. Many of his writings are extant, among them compilations, commentaries, translations and original works in prose and poetry.

XXIX. QUADRIPARTITUM NUMERORUM OF JEAN DE MEURS.

A 14th century arithmetic in which, although an abacus is employed, the methods are those of the algorists. A manuscript of the work is found in Vienna, and two chapters have been transcribed by Nagl.[2]

The second of these chapters contains about 600 words and treats of the operations with integers. It begins

Capitulum 14m de tabula abaci subtilis computationis.

Jean de Meurs lived in the middle of the 14th century, and though primarily a musician, he was also known as a mathematician. He was one of the first to be interested in the reformation of the calendar. Another arithmetic, theoretical in its content, and based upon that of Boethius, was written by the same author.[3]

[1] The copy read is in the library of the University of Michigan.

[2] *Das Quadripartitum des Joannes de Muris und das practisches Rechnen im vierzehnten Jahrhundert, Abh. zur Gesch. der Math. V, pp. 136–146.*

[3] Cf. D. E. Smith, *Rara Arithmetica, p. 117.*

XXX. AN ENGLISH ALGORISM OF THE FOURTEENTH CENTURY.[1]

This is evidently a commentary on the *Carmen de Algorismo.* Professor D. E. Smith has made a study of the work and has published three pages in fac-simile with a transcription and notes on the same.[2] The fragment printed treats only of numeration, but the work considers also the zero, addition, subtraction and multiplication. The manuscript is evidently incomplete.

XXXI. A TREATISE ON NUMERATION OF ALGORISM.

A work published by James Orchard Halliwell in his *Rara Mathematica, 1839.*[3] The manuscript was in his own library, and he places the date in the 14th century. It is written in English and contains about 550 words, the content dealing with numeration only.

XXXII. ALGORISMUS PROSAYCUS MAGISTRI CHRISTANI.

An algorithm based upon the work of Sacrobosco. The manuscript, which is in the library of the University of Prague, was transcribed by F. J. Studniçke and printed in 1893. (*Algorismus prosaycus magistri Christani anno fere 1400 scriptus. Nunc primum edidit Dr. F. J. Studniçke c. r. prof. math. publ. ord. universitatis litterarium bohem etc., Pragae, 1893.*[4] It contains about 3500 words, beginning

> *Motus parvulorum amore rudimenta artis composite brevi stilo curavi conscribere.*

and ending

> . . . *tunc tantum valet ut ille minucie sicut integrum sicut* (*sic*) *unius halensis vel ulne valent 1 integrum halensem vel vlnam*[5] . . .

Christanus Prachticensis (1368–1439) was a teacher at Prague.

[1] Referred to hereafter as *An English algorism.*

[2] *An ancient English algorism, Archiv für Gesch. d. Naturwissen, und der Technik, I, pp. 301–309.*

[3] The copy read is in the library of the University of Michigan.

[4] Published *also in Sitzungsberichte der Königl. Böhmischen Gesellschaft der Wissenschaften. VI, 1893,* to be found in the Library of Congress.

[5] Cf. Cantor, *Zeitschr. fur Math. und Phys. Vol. 38 (1893), Hist. Abt. pp. 198–199.*

XXXIII. ALGORISMUS DE INTEGRIS OF PROSDOCIMO DE BELDAMANDI.[1]

A treatise of about 15000 words, dealing with the fundamental operations with integers. Its similarity to the *Algorismus Vulgaris* of Sacrobosco is striking, and that the author was also a student of Euclid and Boethius is shown by his frequent references to their works. The algorism, which was written in 1410, was edited by Federicus Delphinus in 1534, who "corrected some mistakes" and "added some words for the sake of clearness," but undoubtedly in all essentials the printed arithmetic is the work of Beldamandi. After an introduction by Delphinus, the algorism begins;

Inveni in q̄ pluribus libris algorismi nuncupatis modos operandi circa numeros satis varios . . .

and ends

Volentibus alium modum operandi in hac arte quam istum studeant se exercere in algorismo Joannis de Sacrobosco.

Finis Algorismi de integris magistri Prodocimi de Beldamandis Pataui.

Beldamandi was an Italian scholar of the early 15th century. He was educated at Padua and was made Professor of Astrology in that university in 1422. He died in 1428.

XXXIV. THE ALGORISM OF JOHN KILLINGWORTH.

An arithmetic written in 1444, following closely the methods of Sacrobosco. The manuscript, which is unique, is in the library of the University of Cambridge, and an analysis of its contents has been made by L. C. Karpinski.[2]

This algorism is divided into three parts treating of operations with integers, operations with sexagesimal fractions and tables. It begins

Incipit prohemium in Algorismum Magistri Joannis Kyllyngokorth: Obliuione raro traduntur quo certo convertuntur ordine.

John Killingworth was a distinguished astronomer and mathematician of Merton College, Oxford. The date of his death is given as May 15, 1445.

[1] The copy read is the 1540 edition, lent from the library of G. A. Plimpton.

[2] *The algorism of John Killingworth*, to appear in the *Eng. Hist. Rev.*

XXXV. A FIFTEENTH CENTURY ALGORISM.

An anonymous work, the manuscript of which is in Vienna. In a recent article[1] Dr. E. Rath has published a description of its contents and has compared it with the *Bamberg Arithmetic*[2] and with the *Algorismus Ratisponensis*.[3] The conclusion drawn is that this work, and also the Bamberg Arithmetic are based upon the *Algorismus Ratisponensis.* It treats of the operations upon integers and fractions, proportion and practical applications; and as in the *Algorismus Ratisponensis,* the work on integers resembles that of Sacrobosco.

XXXVI. A GERMAN ALGORISM.

An elementary treatise written in low German, probably about 1445, by Bernhard, a member of the Hildesheim chapter school. The manuscript is now in the University Library in Basel, and was transcribed and translated into modern German by Friedrich Unger.[4] The work contains about 3500 words and treats of the fundamental operations with integers. Though written in German, the technical terms are in Latin.

XXXVII. THE ARITHMETIC OF AL-KALCADI.

An Arabic arithmetic translated into French from a manuscript in the possession of Reinaud by F. Woepcke.[5] The work contains an introduction, four parts, and a conclusion, and the title is *The lifting of the veil from the Gobar science.*[6] In the introduction is given a short account of numeration. The first part deals with operations upon integers, the decomposition of numbers into factors, denomination and proofs.

[1] *Über ein deutsches Rechenbuch aus 15 Jahrhundert, Bibl. Math.* 13_3 *p. 17–22.*

[2] A German arithmetic published in 1482, see Smith, *Rara Arithmetica p. 12.*

[3] An algorism copied and perhaps written by Frater Fredricus of the Cloister Emerams in Regensberg. In the article mentioned above, it is stated that Max. Curtze left a transcription of the algorism ready to print.

[4] *Zeitschr. für Math. und Phys.* XXXIII, *Hist. Abt,* p. 125–145.

[5] *Atti delle' Accad. pont. de' nuovi Lincei* XII, p. 230–275, 399–438.

[6] In other manuscripts it is called *Revelation of secrets in the employment of Gobar signs,* and *Lifting the cover of the science of calculation.* See *Journal Asiatique,* IV_6, *p. 359–360.*

Part two is concerned with fractions, and part three with roots. Part four has for its title *The determination of the unknown*, and among other subjects considers the solution of the quadratic equation. The conclusion is chiefly concerned with series.

Al-Kalçadi was an Arabic mathematician of Spain. He died in 1486.

XXXVIII. ELEMENTA ARITHMETICA ALGORITHMUS DE NUMERIS AUCTORE GEORGIO PEURBACHIO.[1]

An arithmetic written about the middle of the 15th century. It was first printed in 1492, and afterward went through many editions.[2] The fact that this work was widely used in the schools and universities of Germany, made it an influential factor in determining the character of the 16th century arithmetic.

The work is written in Latin and contains about 9000 words. It treats of the fundamental operations with integers and fractions, proportion and rule of false position.

It begins

Numerum Mathematici tripartiuntur.

and ends with the words

Alia fac similia, quae omnia venuste habes circa praecedentem Algorithmum igitur sufficiant.

George von Peurbach (1423–1461) studied and taught in Vienna. He is known chiefly as an astronomer, and as the teacher of Regiomontanus.

[1] The copy read is the 1534 edition, from the library of L. C. Karpinski.
[2] Smith, *Rara Arith.* p. 53.

SECTION III.

The Fundamental Operations.

As might be expected in treatises covering a period of eight centuries, there is little uniformity in the choice of fundamental operations. Some were written for the use of readers already familiar with the numeral system, and others to introduce that system where it was practically unknown. It is natural that the writers of the first class should be concerned with the applications, and that those of the latter class should devote their attention to the processes of calculation.

In the Hindu works the science of computation, or *ganita*, includes both arithmetic and mensuration[1] and consequently we find in Brahmagupta's *Ganitad'hyaya* twenty operations, though Mahaviracarya and Bhaskara omit those dealing with mensuration, and limit the number to eight. Among the Hindus numeration never appears except as a list of names for the powers of ten, and addition and subtraction are treated only in connection with series. In adapting the Hindu learning to the needs of the court at Bagdad, Al-Khowarizmi omitted the work on mensuration and included an extended treatment of the number system. To the arithmetical operations already found in the Hindu works, he added duplation and mediation, and through the translations of his arithmetic, these were introduced into Europe where they were retained as separate operations by many writers throughout the sixteenth century. Al-Nasawi and Al-Hassar also included duplation and mediation among the operations, but the more extended and scientific treatises of Al-Karkhi, Al-Banna and Al-Kalcadi make no mention of them.

A peculiarity found in some of the Arabic arithmetics[2] is the introduction of the operation of *denomination*, or

[1] Cf. G. R. Kaye, *Hindu Mathematical Methods*. *Bibl. Math.* XI$_3$, p. 293.

[2] Cf. IX, XX, XXXVII.

division of a smaller by a larger number, which does not appear in the Hindu works or the Latin algorisms, though *denominatio* is used commonly by the abacists to indicate a quotient.

The Latin works begin invariably with a discussion of the number system, though numeration is not always considered one of the arithmetical operations. The earlier works have no general term to include these operations, and it is difficult to determine their number, but that numeration was regarded somewhat differently from the others, at least in the *Liber algorismi de pratica arismetrice,* is shown by the headings of the chapters. Alexander de Villa Dei states distinctly that there are seven *parts* to algorism, and John of Sacrobosco gives nine *species*. It is one of the many evidences of their influence, that in general, later treatises adopt one of these statements, though some, among them the *Speculum doctrinale* of Vincent de Beauvais, name only six.[1]

Thus it will be seen that a choice of fundamental operations based on the works examined must be an arbitrary one. In the present section an attempt has been made to show what operations the author of each treatise considered fundamental, but the sections to follow will discuss only those contained in the Latin translation of the arithmetic of Al-Khowarizmi, namely, the four operations of *addition*, *subtraction*, *multiplication* and *division*, which the arithmetician of today considers fundamental, together with *numeration*, *duplation* and *mediation*.

I. BRAHMAGUPTA.

Brahmagupta states that "he who distinctly and severally knows addition, and the rest of the *twenty* logistics, and the *eight* determinations including measurement by shadow, is a mathematician." The commentary by Chaturveda explains that the twenty logistics (*paracarman*), or arithmetical

[1] For this information I am indebted to Professor L. C. Karpinski, who has made a study of this work, and who states that the work is not an algorism, but contains a chapter in which is considered the method of writing numbers. The operations are mentioned only incidentally.

operations, are *addition*, *subtraction*, *multiplication*, *division*, *square*, *square root*, *cube*, *cube root*, *six rules for the reduction of fractions*, *rule of three*, *rule of five*, *of seven*, *of nine* and *of eleven*, and *barter;* and that the eight determinations are *mixture*, *progression*, *plane figures*, *excavation*, *stack*, *saw*, *mound* and *shadow*.

II. ALGORITMI DE NUMERO INDORUM.

There is no general term to include all the arithmetical operations, but in that part of the treatise dealing with integers the author considers in the following order: *numeration*, *addition*, *subtraction*, *mediation*, *duplation*, *multiplication* and *division*. The original work of which this is a translation, must have contained also an explanation of the *extraction of roots*, for this statement is made, "*And now we will begin to treat of multiplication and division of fractions, and the extraction of roots.*[1]

III. MAHAVIRACARYA.

There are eight operations of arithmetic (called *parikarman*), namely; *multiplication*, *division*, *square*, *square root*, *cube*, *cube root*, *summation of series*, and *Vyutkalita*, by which is meant the finding of the sum of a part of a series after a certain number of terms have been cut off from the beginning.

IV. IBN LABBAN.

The subjects considered are *numeration*, *addition*, *subtraction*, *multiplication*, *division*, *extraction of roots*, and the *check by nines*.

V. SRIDHARACARYA.

There is no general term to indicate the arithmetical operations, but all the subjects mentioned in I appear in this work.

[1] *Et nunc incipiemus tractare de multiplicatione fractionum, et earum divisione, et de extractione radicum*, Trattati I, p. 17.

VI. AL-NASAWI.

No general term is used to indicate the operations, but the work treats of *numeration, addition, duplation, subtraction, mediation, multiplication, division, square root, cube root.*

Beginning with the case of addition, each operation except those of duplation and mediation occupies two chapters, the first of which describes the process and the second the proof. For mediation and duplation there is no chapter describing the process, a fact which together with the order of the operations, seems to indicate that duplation may have been considered as a species of addition, and mediation as a species of subtraction.

VII. AVICENNA.

In the fragment translated, there is a paragraph on numeration, followed by the proofs (*check by nines*) for *addition, subtraction, multiplication,* and *division.*

VIII. AL-KARKHI.

The *Kâfi fîl Hisâb* was not written to introduce the Hindu methods of calculation. It gives many different methods for *multiplication* and *division*, and an extended treatment of the *extraction of roots* and of their approximation.

IX. AL-HASSAR.

The work on integers treats of *numeration, addition, subtraction, multiplication, denomination, division, mediation, duplation, square root.*

X. BHASKARA.

In the *Lilavati* it is stated that there are eight operations of arithmetic (*paracarmashtaca*) namely; *addition, subtraction, multiplication, division, square, square root, cube, cube root.* In the *VijaGanita*, a work on algebra, the same operations with the exception of *cube* and *cube root* appear.[1]

[1] In his article on *Hindu Mathematical methods, Bibl. Math. XI₃, p. 293,* C. R. Kaye states that Bhaskara speaks of thirty operations, which he thinks may include the operations and determinations of Brahmagupta together with trigonometry and indeterminate equations.

XI. LIBER ALGORISMI.

The work, an algorism, is divided into chapters each with its own heading. Under the title *Incipit liber algoarismi de pratica arismetrice*, is a long and complete description of *numeration*. This is followed by chapters on *addition*, *subtraction*, *duplation*, *mediation*, *multiplication* and *division of* integers introduced by the words, *Regule de Scientia agregandi*, *Regule de Scientia dimenuendi* etc. After several chapters dealing with fractions there follows an explanation of *square root*.

XII. A TWELFTH CENTURY ALGORISM.

After the introduction, the treatise contains a short discussion of the units of time and of the Hindu numerals, but it is evident that numeration is not considered one of the fundamental operations. These are *multiplication*, *addition*, *subtraction*, *mediation*, *duplation* and *division*. The work also considers *square root*.

XIII. RAOUL DE LAON.

The work opens with an extended description of the abacus and the number system employed. This is followed by an explanation of *multiplication*, *addition*, *subtraction*, and *division*.

XIV. ABRAHAM BEN ESRA.

This treatise states that there are seven arithmetical operations, namely, *multiplication*, *division*, *addition*, *subtraction*, *fractions*, *proportion* and *square root*.

XV. DEMONSTRATIO JORDANI DE ALGORISMO.

This work begins with a series of definitions concerning number, but *numeration* is not defined. There follow definitions of *addition*, *subtraction*, *duplation*, *mediation*, *multiplication*, *division* and *extraction of (square) root*.

XVI. LEONARD OF PISA.

In chapters I–VII of the *Liber abaci*, we find *numeration*, *multiplication*, *addition*, *subtraction*, and *division*. Chapter XIV deals with *square* and *cube roots*.

XVII. ALEXANDER DE VILLA DEI.

Here it is stated that there are seven parts (*partes*) to the science of algorism, namely; *addition*, *subtraction*, *duplation*, *mediation*, *multiplication*, *division*, and *extraction of* (*square and cube*) *roots*.

XVIII. SACROBOSCO.

In the *Algorismus Vulgaris*, the word *species*, which was so commonly used in later works, appears for the first time as a generic term for the arithmetical operations. In this work there are nine of these *species* namely; *numeration*, *addition*, *subtraction*, *mediation*, *duplation*, *multiplication*, *division*, *progression* and the *extraction of* (*square and cube*) *roots*.

XIX. SALEM CODEX.

The word *species* is used as a general name for the operations, of which there are seven,[1] namely; *addition*, *subtraction*, *duplation*, *mediation*, *division*, and *extraction of* (*square and cube*) *roots*.

XX. AL-BANNA.

There is no general name for the operations, but in the treatise are found *numeration*, *addition*, *subtraction*, *multiplication*, *division*, and *denomination*. After the work on fractions, Al-Banna explains *square root*.

XXI. OCREATUS.

The treatise considers only *multiplication* and *division*, preceded by a short explanation of *numeration*.

[1] Cf. XVII "*Septem sunt partes, non plures, istius artis*"; *Carmen de Algorismo*. "*Huius disciplinae non plures quam VII habentur species.*" *Salem Codex.*

XXII. ALGORITHMUS DEMONSTRATUS.

No general name is used for the operations, but both *species* and *operationes* are used in the work. The operations considered are *addition, subtraction, duplation, mediation, multiplication, division, square root, cube root.*

XXIII. A FRENCH ALGORISM.

This algorism says "*6 parties sont d'augorism*" but it mentions *addition, subtraction, duplation, mediation, multiplication, division, extraction of (square and cube) roots.*

XXIV. A THIRTEENTH CENTURY ALGORISM.

Six operations (*modus docendorum*) are mentioned namely; *addition, subtraction, multiplication, division, extraction of roots, fractions.*

XXV. PETRUS DE DACIA.

Same as XVIII.

XXVI. LEWI BEN GERSON.

The subjects considered are *addition, subtraction, multiplication, series, permutations, combinations, division, proportion, square* and *cube root.*

XXVII. AN ICELANDIC ALGORISM.

Same as XVII.

XXVIII. PLANUDES.

The work begins with a dissertation on number, followed by chapters describing *addition, subtraction, multiplication,* and *division.* The discussion of *square root* is inserted after the work on fractions.

XXXII. ALGORISMUS PROSAYCUS.

There are nine *species;* namely *numeration, addition, subtraction, mediation, duplation, multiplication, division, progression* and *extraction of (square and cube) roots.*

XXXIII. BELDAMANDI.

This treatise states that there are nine *species* or *operationes*, namely; *numeration*, *addition*, *subtraction*, *mediation*, *duplation*, *multiplication*, *division*, *progression*, *extraction of (square and cube) roots.*

XXXIV. KILLINGWORTH.

Here the word *species* is used as a generic name for the operations, of which there are seven, namely; *addition*, *subtraction*, *duplation*, *mediation*, *multiplication*, *division*, *square root.*

XXXV. A FIFTEENTH CENTURY ALGORISM.

In this work the operations considered are *numeration*, *addition*, *subtraction*, *multiplication*, and *division*. *Mediation* appears as a special case of *division*.

XXXVI. A GERMAN ALGORISM.

Here it is stated that algorism is divided into seven parts, namely; *addition*, *subtraction*, *duplation*, *mediation*, *multiplication*, *division*, and *extraction of (square and cube) roots.*

XXXVII. AL-KALCADI.

In the introduction is given a short account of *numeration*. Chapters I–VI consider *addition*, *subtraction*, *multiplication*, *division*, and *denomination*. In the third part of the treatise are found *extraction of square root* and *methods of approximation*.

XXVIII. PEURBACH.

This work begins with a discussion of *numeration*, and then considers the operations of *addition*, *subtraction*, *mediation*, *duplation*, *multiplication* and *division*, which are called *species*.

SECTION IV.

Numeration.

The necessity for a chapter on numeration in the Hindu works on arithmetic is obviated by the fact that a knowledge of the numerals antedates any existing treatise by so long a period that it was regarded by their authors as of divine origin.[1] Hence we find in these treatises only a list of names proceeding to high powers of ten. Among the Arabs, however, especially in the later works, there is introduced an extended discussion of numeration. These writers make no attempt to name the orders higher than thousands, and the twelve *names* given by Al-Karkhi suffice for any number however great. The method of reading numbers by thousands, introduced into Europe by the Latin translations of the Arabic works, persisted throughout the period under consideration, and even into the 16th century.

In the Latin algorisms traces of the Greek influence are evident. The conception of number as a collection of units, though unity itself is not a number, is Greek rather than Hindu, and the distinction between *odd* and *even*, and *prime* and *composite* numbers as well as the idea of *related* numbers may be traced to the same source. The division into *digits*, *articles* and *mixed* numbers, appearing almost without exception in algorisms of the 13th century or later was probably due to the work of Boethius to whom reference is sometimes made, but it is possible that this division, as found in the *Liber algorismi de pratica arismetrice*, a treatise based upon Arabic sources, may be due to the work of Al-Khowarizmi.[2]

[1] Bhaskara says "the invention of nine figures with device of place being ascribed to the beneficent Creator of the universe."

[2] Eneström states, on the authority of Suter that the word *'iqd* is sometimes used by Al-Khowarizmi to denote a multiple of ten, *Bibl. Math.* IX_3, *p. 350*, and the use of *nodi* from *uqud* in the same sense, was found by Karpinski in the translation of Al-Khowarizmi's algebra by Robert of Chester, *Bibl. Math.* IX_3, *p. 129*.

Digits are universally the numbers less than ten. Articles are generally the multiples of ten, powers of ten receiving the special designation of *limits*, but the *Salem Codex* admits only powers of ten, and the *Algorithmus Demonstratus* numbers of the form $a.10^n$. Mixed numbers are defined sometimes as numbers lying between adjacent articles, and sometimes as combinations of articles and digits, both definitions appearing in the work of Sacrobosco.

Most of the Latin writers distinguish between the *nine* numerals and the zero, which is only a symbol to designate a vacant place, but the *Carmen de algorismo,* and the works based upon it, refer to the *ten* Hindu numerals. *Figura* is the word appearing ordinarily for one of the nine digits, though the translation of Al-Khowarizmi's arithmetic uses also *litera* and *caracter*, the latter being the term applied to the numerals drawn upon the apices of Gerbert. Zero in the earliest works is designated by *circulus*, but generally in the later treatises by some form of *cyfra*, and the use of the symbol is always explained with great care. The orders are usually indicated by *differentia* though *mansio, limes, gradus, locus* and *ordo* are terms occasionally used in the same sense. The decuple ratio of the orders is emphasized in most of the treatises and frequently a large number is given as illustration, the order and name of each digit as well as the method of reading and writing it being carefully explained.

II. ALGORITMI DE NUMERO INDORUM.

Term. tech.: *litera, figura, caracter* = one of the nine numerals; *circulus* = zero; *differentia, mansio* = order. Unity is the base of all number, but not itself a number.[1] A number is a collection of units. All numbers of units order are formed by *doubling* and *tripling* unity, all numbers of the tens order by *doubling* and *tripling* ten, etc. The orders proceed in decuple ratio. Zero is used to designate a vacant order (*ut per hoc scirent quod differentia esset vacua*).

[1] This statement is made also in the algebra of Al-Khowarizmi, to which reference is made.

About half the work on numeration is devoted to an explanation of the method of writing and reading numbers. Though the number is not written in the new system, the writer explains the method of reading *1,180,073,051,492,863*.

III. MAHAVIRACARYA.

Hindu names are given for the first 24 orders.

V. SRIDHARACARYA.

Hindu names are given for the first 18 orders.

VI. AL-NASAWI.

The analysis states that this work explains the forms of numerals, and the Hindu method of writing numbers.

VIII. AL-KARKHI.

In connection with number are mentioned: *orders,* all of which depend upon three, *units, tens* and *hundreds,* and are formed by combining with these, *thousands,* repeated as often as desired, *order-units,* which are the digits 1–9, *names,* of which there are 12, viz. *one, two* . . . *ten, hundred* and *thousand.*

IX. AL-HASSAR.

The 12 *names* as in VIII. Unity is the origin of number, and is the *index* of the units, as ten is the index of the tens etc. Each number of an order is found by continued addition of the index to itself.

X. BHASKARA.

Numbers increase by multiples of ten. Names are given for the first 18 orders.

XI. LIBER ALGORISMI.

Term. tech.: *figurae,* = the nine numerals; *circulus* = zero (*ciffre* and *siffre* are found in one of the excerpts in the latter half of the book. (Trattati II, p. 113, 114)); *limites* = powers of ten; *differentiae,* = orders; *digiti* = numbers less than 10; *articuli* = multiples of ten except powers of ten; *compositi* = numbers between the articles.

The work on numeration resembles that of II. Unity is the base of number, number is a collection of units. Numbers of each order are formed by *doubling* and *tripling* the first. Place value and the use of the zero are explained as in II. No explanation of the method of reading numbers is given, but it is clear that the orders proceed by thousands in groups of three.[1] In one of the excerpts (p. 123) the method for determining the order of a digit is given as follows. Multiply by three the number of times *thousand* is repeated, and add *one, two* or *three* according as those thousands are multiplied by *units, tens* or *hundreds.*

XII. A TWELFTH CENTURY ALGORISM.

Term. tech.: *figurae* = the nine numerals; *ciffra* = zero: *species* = three divisions of numbers (1) numbers less than ten, (2) multiples of ten, (3) numbers composed of both (1) and (2); *differentia* = order. A brief explanation of the ratio of the orders is given.

XIV. ABRAHAM BEN ESRA.

A short discussion of number appears in the introductory paragraph. Numbers of the form $a.10^n$, $a.10^{n+m}$ . . . . are *similar* numbers. *Nine* Hindu numbers are given with their Hebrew equivalents, and the tenth is called a *wheel* or "*Sifra in the foreign speech.*" The writer gives an explanation of the decimal system and the method of writing numbers, but it is evident that some knowledge of the subject is presupposed.

XV. DEMONSTRATIO JORDANI DE ALGORISMO.

Term. tech.: *figurae* = the nine numerals; *sciffula, scifula* = zero; *differentia* (*limes* used once) = orders; *digitus* =

[1] *Nonum (limitem) vero, centies millies millium, Decionum vero, millies mille millium*—p. 26.

number less than ten; *articulus* = a multiple of ten; *compositus numerus* = a number represented by several digits; *numerus simplex* = a number of the form $a.10^n$, when $a<10$; *numeri similes* = numbers of the form $a.10^n$, $a.10^{n+m}$. There is nothing in this work which could be called a discussion of numeration.

XVI. LEONARD OF PISA.

Term. tech.: *figurae* = the nine numerals; *zephyrum* = zero; *gradus* = order. No attempt is made to define unity, but number is defined as a collection of units. The decuple ratio of the orders is explained, and the effect of interchanging digits is illustrated. The orders proceed by thousands, and in writing large numbers the groups are separated by arcs (*virgula in modum arcus*). The example given is

$$678\overset{\frown}{935}\overset{\frown}{784}\overset{\frown}{105}\overset{\frown}{296}.$$

The chapter on numeration closes with an account of finger symbolism, necessary because in many cases a number must be "*held in the hand.*"

Inserted in the chapter on division is a distinction between *prime* and *composite* numbers. The prime numbers which here are called *numeri sine regulis*, Leonard states are called *hassam* among the Arabs, and *coris canon* among the Greeks.

XVII. ALEXANDER DE VILLA DEI.

Term. tech.: *figurae* = the *ten* Hindu numerals; *cifra* = zero; *species* = the three divisions of numbers into digits, articles and composite numbers; *digiti* = the numbers less than ten; *articuli* = multiples of ten; *compositi* = numbers composed of digits and articles.

Six lines are devoted to an explanation of the method of writing numbers. The statement is made that a number is *odd* or *even* according as the units digit is odd or even.

XVIII. SACROBOSCO.

The introductory paragraph in this work begins with an appreciation of number taken from Boethius and Aristotle.

"*All things,*" he says "*which have originated from the beginning have been formed by means of a science of number, and to whatever extent all things exist they must be so recognized, since the science of numbering has been allied with universal knowledge.*"[1] *Number* is defined as a collection of units, and a *unit* that by which *one* exists.

Term. tech.: *digitus* = a number less than ten; *articulus* = a multiple of ten; *numerus compositus, numerus mixtus* = a number composed of an article and a digit, or a number lying between two adjacent articles. The first of the nine *species* is numeration which is defined as follows: *Numeration* (*numeratio*) *is the representing of any number by appropriate figures, according to the rules of the science.* It is stated that *figura, differentia, locus* and *limes* signify the same, but are used under different circumstances: *figura* when referring to the geometrical delineation by lines; *differentia* when referring to the ratio of one digit to the proceeding; *locus* when referring to the space in which it is written, and *limes* when referring to the ordered way of writing a number. It is stated that there are nine *limits* corresponding to the nine significant figures, but Sacrobosco's use of the word *limit* is not clear. In his chapter on the extraction of roots, he explains that the first limit includes the nine digits, and that the second, third and fourth represent the even tens, hundreds and thousands. The statement is made that the 5th, 6th and 7th limits are formed by combining digits with the 2nd, 3rd, and 4th, but it is impossible to discover from the text what meaning he assigned to the 8th and 9th. In the commentary by Petrus de Dacia (No. XXV), we find that author's interpretation.[2]

Sacrobosco distinguishes between the nine significant figures (*figurae significativae*) and the zero (*teca, cyfra, figura*

[1] *Omnia, quae a primaeva rerum origine processerunt, ratione numerorum formata sunt, et quemadmodum sunt, sic cognosci habent: unde in universa rerum cognitione est ars numerandi cooperativa.*

[2] The text in the *Algorismus vulgaris* is as follows: *Tres (limites) etiam resultant in compositis per digitorum appositionem super quemcumque trium praedictorum, et si alter alteri praeponatur. Sed per finalis termini replicationem supra se semel per modum quadratorum aut bispermodum solidorum quocumque alio praecedente resultat penultimus limes et ultimus.* p. 15.

nichili). He explains place value, and suggests that dots be placed above the fourth, and every succeeding third figure to indicate the number of thousands.

XIX. SALEM CODEX.

Term. tech.: *figurae* = the nine Hindu numerals; *cifra* = zero; *digiti* = numbers less than ten; *articuli* = powers of ten; *compositi* = numbers made up of articles and digits; *differentia*, *locus* = order.

Number is defined as a collection of units, but unity is not a number. The numbers 2 and 3 are developed by doubling and tripling unity,[1] and the other digits by multiplication, duplication or addition of these; i.e. 4 and 9 are formed by multiplication of 2 by 2, and of 3 by 3; 5 and 7 by the addition of 2 to 3, and of 3 to 4; 6, 8, 10 by doubling 3, 4, 5.

Place value is explained. Numbers are divided by points into groups of three figures, and in reading, the word thousand is repeated as many times as there are points. As an illustration we find 495.827.361.052.951. Though the Hindu numerals are used for the illustrative examples, all explanations are made with Roman numbers.

XX. AL-BANNA.

All numbers are composed of units.[2] As in the arithmetic of Nikomachus, numbers are *even* or *odd*, the even numbers being *even*, *evenly uneven*, and *evenly even and uneven*,[3] and the odd numbers being *prime* or *composite*.

The orders are designated by a word translated *habitations* which suggests the *mansio* of II. The twelve *names* appear as in VIII and IX, and the rule for finding the place of a digit is given as in XI.

[1] Cf. II and XI.

[2] The translator states in a note that the numbers 1–9 are meant by the *units*, but it seems probable that Al-Banna was defining number as a *collection of units*.

[3] That is, powers of 2, doubles of uneven numbers, and other even numbers.

XXI. OCREATUS.

The work on numeration which is incomplete, is taken from XI, as a few lines will show.

From XI. *Ordines vero siui limites numerorum a primis numeris, qui digiti uocantur, et sunt .9. per decuplos in infinitum procedunt. Unde in unoquoque limite numerorum sunt termini .9. nec plures excogitari possunt. Omnes autem, qui sunt in ceteris limitibus, preter primum, articuli solent appellari. Ut sit primus limes ab uno us que ad .10. etc.* (p. 27. *Boncompagni Trattati II*).

From XXI. *Ordines igitur numerorum sivi limites a primis numeris qui digiti vocantur et sunt. IX. per decuplos in infinitum procedunt. Sunt autem in unoquoque limite numerorum novem termini, nec plures inveniri vel excogitari possunt. . . . . Omnes autem qui sunt in caeteris limitibus, praeter primum, articuli solent appellari: ut sit primus limes ab I usque ad X etc.* (*Abh. zur Gesch. der Math. III p. 132.*)

The paragraph proceeds to state that each order is ten times the preceding.

XXII. ALGORITHMUS DEMONSTRATUS.

The treatise opens with a set of definitions and axioms divided into three groups under the headings, *Descriptiones, Conceptiones, Petitiones.*

In the first group *digiti* = numbers less than ten; *articuli* = numbers of the form $a.10^n$, $a<10$; *numeri compositi* = numbers containing more than one significant figure; *numeri relatavi* = numbers of the form $a.10^n$ and $a.10^{n+m}$; *limes* = order.

In the second group it is stated that each order is ten times the preceding, and that the rank of a number in any order is the quotient of that number by the first number of the order, an axiom of which use is made frequently in the succeeding pages.

In the third group, *figurae* = the nine numerals; *cifra, circulus, figura nichili* = zero.

XXIII. A FRENCH ALGORISM.

This work contains nothing not found in the *Carmen de algorismo.* The technical terms resemble those in the Latin work, *figure* = the ten numerals; *cyfra* = zero; *degit, digit* = numbers less than ten; *article* = a multiple of ten; *compost* = numbers composed of digits and articles.

XXIV. A THIRTEENTH CENTURY ALGORISM.

Term. tech.: *figurae* = the nine numerals; *cyfre* = zero; *digiti* = numbers less than ten; *articuli* = multiples of ten; *numerī compositi* = numbers composed of articles and digits; *limites* = articles which are powers of ten.

Place value is explained very briefly. Roman numerals are used in the text.

XXV. PETRUS DE DACIA.

Points to be noted in the commentary on the *Algorismus vulgaris* are the explanation of the word *teca*, used for the zero, and the interpretation of *limes*. The zero, it is stated, resembles the circular iron, or *teca*, used for branding criminals, and hence its name.[1]

According to Sacrobosco's definition of limits, one would assume the 5th, 6th, and 7th limits to include numbers of the forms 10a + b, 100a + b, when *a* and *b* are any of the nine digits, and so the commentary explains the meaning at first, but continues "*Sed addit auctor, quod est, si alter alteri praeponatur, resultabit aliquis de his tribus limitibus.*" This Dacia explains as meaning that the 5th limit shall be formed by combining the digits with the principal articles and shall include all the numbers between ten and a hundred, except multiples of ten; that the 6th limit shall be formed by combining the digits and principal articles with the hundreds and shall include all numbers between 100 and 1000 except multiples of 100; and that similarly the 7th limit shall be

[1] This name might also be a corruption of *theta*, since we frequently find the zero written θ. Cf. *Bibl. Math* I_2, p. 120.

formed by combining all the hundreds, tens and digits with the thousands, and shall include all the numbers between 1000 and 10000 except multiples of thousands. The eighth limit he understands to include all multiples of 1000 from 1,000,000 to 9,000,000, and the ninth to include all multiples of 1,000,000 from 1,000,000,000 to 9,000,000,000.[1] As an example of the method of writing numbers this work gives $\dot{9}87\dot{6}54\dot{3}210$.

XXVI. LEWI BEN GERSON.

Unity is defined as the base of all numbers, but is not itself a number. Without unity no number could exist, but unity could exist alone. Number is unlimited above and below, unity being the common origin.[2]

XXVIII. PLANUDES.

This work begins with a description of the nine numerals and the zero, followed by a paragraph on place value, with 8132674592 as an illustration. Attention is called to the fact that zero never stands at the left of a number.

XXX. AN ENGLISH ALGORISM.

As in the *Carmen de algorismo*, this work states that there are ten figures (*figurys*). There follows an explanation of place value with 9634 used as an illustration.

XXXI. A TREATISE ON NUMERATION.

Evidently taken from XXX, as a few lines will show.

From XXX. *loo an ensampull .9.6.3.4 the figr of .4. that hase this schape .4. betokens that hym selfe for he stondes in the first place. The figr of 3. that has this schape .3. betokens ten tymes more than he schuld & he stode th tht the figr of .4. stondes .tht is thretty. etc.*

[1] Cf. Eneström, *Les limites mentionnes dans l'algorismus de Sacrobosco, Bibl. Math.* II_2, p. 97–102.

[2] This does not refer to negative numbers but to fractions. The author states later that unity may be divided into 60 parts, these again into 60 parts, etc.

From XXXI. *lo an axample as thus 9634. This figure of foure that has this schape 4 tokeneth but himself for he stondeth in the first place. The figure of thre that hath this schape 3 tokeneth ten tyme himself for he stondeth in the secunde place and that is thritti. etc.*

XXXII. ALGORISMUS PROSAYCUS.

Sacrobosco's appreciation of number is abridged to the sentence "*Et quia omnis comparaciones summa numero exercetur, igitur a numero tamquam a priori inchoandum est.*" Number is defined as a collection of units, and unity is anything that may be called *one.*

Term. tech.: *digittus* = a number less than ten; *articulus* = a multiple of ten; *numerus compositus,* or *numerus mixtus* = a number composed of an article and a digit; *figurae* = the nine digits; *cifra* = zero; *locus* or *differentia* = order.

XXXIII. BELDAMANDI.

Beldamandi quotes from Euclid and Boethius the definition of number as a collection of unities, but states that he will consider unity a number. (*Et isto modo acciptur numerus in processu huius libelli in quo unitas appellabitur numerus.*)

Term. tech.: *figurae* = the ten numerals; *figure significantes, digiti* = numbers less than ten; *figura nihil, cifra* = zero; *ordo* = order; *articuli* = multiples of ten; *numerus compositus, numerus mixtus* = numbers composed of articles and digits. In reading, numbers proceed in groups of three by thousands.

XXXVI. A GERMAN ALGORISM.

Though the algorism is written in old German, the technical terms are Latin, or Latin words with German endings: *figuren* = the nine numerals; *cyfer* = zero; *numerus digitus* = a number less than ten; *numerus articulus* = a multiple of ten; *numerus compositus siue mixtus* = a number lying between two articles. Odd and even numbers are not defined but it is stated that a number is *odd* or *even* according as the units digit is odd or even. (Cf. XVII.)

XXXVII. AL-KALCADI.

Numeration is considered in an introductory paragraph and begins with a description of the nine numerals and the zero, followed by a brief explanation of the method of writing numbers.

XXXVIII. PEURBACH.

Term. tech.: *figurae* = the ten numerals; *cifra* = zero; *digiti* = numbers less than ten; *articuli* = multiples of ten; *compositi* = numbers formed of digits and articles; *differentia* = order.

Unity is not a number, but is the source of number, to which it is related as the point is related to geometrical magnitudes. There is a brief explanation of place value and the suggestion is made that a point be placed over the fourth and every third succeeding figure to indicate the number of thousands.

SECTION V.

Addition.

Addition as the simplest of the combinatory operations, presented few difficulties at this period. Many of the treatises examined make no mention of it as a separate operation, or consider it only in the case of summation of series, but it is found in the Latin works almost without exception.

The process is always defined as a collecting or joining of numbers, in most cases as the joining of *two* numbers, or as was the custom among the abacists, of adding one number to another. Although frequently mention is made of *two or more* or of *several* numbers, it is usually true that two numbers only, designated as the *upper number* and the *lower number*, appear in the description of the process and in the illustrative examples. Of all the Latin treatises examined, the *Liber abaci* alone of those written before the 15th century uses more than two addends, but the Hebrew work of Lewi ben Gerson is quite advanced in its treatment of the subject.

The reason for the limitation to two numbers is to be found in the strong influence of the abacists, and to this influence is due also the custom of writing the greater number above and replacing it by the sum, and of beginning the addition either at the left or at the right. Usually, though not invariably, the process is considered in three cases: namely, when the sum of the digits of any order is a digit, an article or a composite number, and the method of transferring the article to the order on the left is laboriously explained.

No addition tables are found in these works except in the *Liber abaci* where the sums of all digits, and of the articles up to 90 + 90 are given. As proofs, the check by nines and the reverse operation of subtraction appear with about equal frequency, and Al-Banna mentions also the checks by eights and by sevens.

II. ALGORITMI DE NUMERO INDORUM.

Term. tech.: *addere, colligere, augmentacio.*

Process: Write the numbers, one below the other, units under units, tens under tens, etc. Begin at the left and add the digits of each order.

There is no illustrative example, or proof, and no statement is made as to which number is to be written above, or where the sum is to be placed.

III. MAHAVIRACARYA.

Summation of series only.

V. SRIDHARACARYA.

Summation of series only.

VI. AL-NASAWI.

In the work examined the method is not explained, but it is stated that the result is checked by casting out nines.

VII. AVICENNA.

Process: if you wish to add, collect the different sums.

Example:

```
 1147
  381
16119
 2345
 9123
   58
  611
-----
29784.
```

Note: This example is given in the translation, to illustrate the check by nines, but it is very doubtful if it appeared in the same form in the original manuscript. We may conclude however that Avicenna added more than two numbers.

IX. AL-HASSAR.

It is stated in the work examined, that addition begins at the right, and that the sum is written above.

X. BHASKARA.

Process: "The sum of the figures according to their places is to be taken in the direct or reverse order,[1] or [in the case of subtraction] their difference."

Example: *Dear intelligent Lilavati, if thou be skilled in subtraction and addition, tell me the sum of two, five, thirty-two, a hundred and ninety three, eighteen, ten, and a hundred added together; and the remainder when their sum is subtracted from ten thousand.*

Statement 2, 5, 32, 193, 18, 10, 100.

(Answer) Result of the addition, 360

Statement for subtraction 10000, 360

(Answer) Result of the subtraction 9640.

XI. LIBER ALGORISMI.

Def. To add is to collect two or more numbers into one.

Term. tech.: *agregare, adjungere, colligere, addere, agregatio; numerus cui agregandus, numerus superior; numerus agregandus, numerus inferior.*

Process: The process is explained only for two numbers. Place the greater number above. Begin at the right and let the sum replace the upper number. The treatise states that it is possible to begin at the left.

Example: In the three examples given, the process begins at the right.

For the first, we have the statement	625 586
after addition of units	621 586
after addition of tens.	611 586
final result.	1211

Proof: Check by nines.

[1] Begin either at the right or at the left.

XII. A TWELFTH CENTURY ALGORISM.

Term. tech.: *addere, additio.*

Process: Begin at the right, and add the digits of each order. There is no illustrative example, or proof.

XIV. ABRAHAM BEN ESRA.

The chapter on addition is concerned chiefly with the summation of series, and the addition of degrees, minutes, and seconds, but in one paragraph, there is a description of the process of addition of *two* numbers.

Process: Write the numbers, one below the other, add the digits in each order, and write the sum in a third row.

Proof: Check by nines.

Note: No statement is made as to whether the process begins at the right or left, or whether the sum is placed above or below.

XV. DEMONSTRATIO JORDANI DE ALGORISMO.

Def. To add is to find the sum of two numbers joined together.

Term. tech.:[1] *addere, additio, major numerus, minor numerus, summa, additus, aggregatus.*

Process: Place the greater number above.

There is no illustrative example or proof.

Note: In the work examined it is stated that the process is carried on "*in the usual way.*" It is impossible to say whether this indicates that the process begins at the right or at the left.

XVI. LEONARD OF PISA.

Term. tech.: *additio, collectio, addere, colligere.*

Process: Before describing the last method of multiplication (by a quadrilateral), Leonard introduces a paragraph on addition. Begin at the right and collect "*in manibus,*"

[1] Copied from Eneström's article

the digits of the units order, write the units of the result above the units, and hold the tens in the hand. These must be added with the digits of the tens order, etc.

Examples:

74	4690	511110
25	123	4321
49	4567	506789

Note: In these illustrative examples two numbers only are used, and the greater is always placed below.

Proof: Check by nines.

18542
25
461
6789
58
10718
491

Example: Following the work above, another example is given in which the sum 18542 is written above without the dividing line. The process is described as follows: Add 8 and 1 and 8 and 9 and 1 and 5, always collecting in the hand. This will be 32. Place the 2 and retain the 3, etc.

XVII. ALEXANDER DE VILLA DEI.

Term. tech.: *addere, additio.*

Method: The author adds a number *to* a number. Begin at the right. The sum replaces the upper number.

Proof: By subtraction (*Et subtractio facta tibi probat additionem*).

XVIII. SACROBOSCO.

Def. Addition is the joining of a number, or numbers, to a number, to find a sum.

Term. tech.: *additio, aggregatio, addere; numerus cui debet fiere additio; numerus addendus, summa.*

Process: The work states that it is customary, but not necessary, to write the smaller number below. (*Competentius est, ut minor numeris subscribatur et maiori addatur, quam e contrario; sed sive sic fit, sivi sic, semper idem proveniet.)* Begin at either end, preferably at the right, and write the sum in place of the number which is above.

Proof: By subtraction.

XIX. SALEM CODEX.

Def. Addition is the combination of different numbers into one.

Term. tech.: *additio, addere.*

Process: In the example, the larger number is placed above, though no mention of the relative positions is made in the text. Begin at the right. The sum replaces the upper number.

Example: 666
144.

Proof: Check by nines, or by subtraction.

XX. AL-BANNA.

Def. Addition is the combination of numbers to make a whole.

Process: Al-Banna divides his work on addition into five parts, four of which deal with summation of series. The first of the five divisions considers the addition of two numbers. Begin at the right or the left (preferably at the right). No mention is made of erasure.

Proof: By subtraction. After the chapter on subtraction the checks by nines, eights, and sevens are explained, and the statement is made that these checks may be used to prove the result of addition.

XXII. ALGORITHMUS DEMONSTRATUS.

Def. Addition is the uniting of two numbers into a sum.

Term. tech.: *additio, addere, summa.*

Process: Begin at the right or the left (in the example the process begins at the right). The sum replaces the upper number. The peculiarity in this work is that when in the addition of the digits of any order, an article or composite number arises, the digit in the tens place is actually added to the next digit of the upper number before the addition proceeds.

Example: d c b a o o o
f g h k o o o

In this example we are to suppose that the sum of a and k is 6, and that the sum of b and h is 10, then the 1 from this 10 is added to c. Suppose the sum of 1 and c is 10, then carry the 1 to the d and suppose the sum of 1 and d is 5. The example would stand 5 0 0 6 0 0 0 before the digits
f g h k 0 0 0
of the sixth order are added.[1]

Proof: By subtraction.

XXIII. A FRENCH ALGORISM.

Term. tech.: *assembler*.

Process: Write the greater number above. Begin at the right, and replace the upper number by the sum.

No example or proof is given.

XXIV. A THIRTEENTH CENTURY ALGORISM.

Def. To add is to join a number to a number.

Term. tech.: *addidere, jungere, adjungere, conjungere, aggregare; major numerus; minor numerus; summa.*

Process: Write the greater number above. Begin to add at the right, and replace the upper number by the sum.

Example: 861
741
The result is 1602
741
No proof is given.

[1] This is exactly what would occur if one were using an abacus.

XXV. PETRUS DE DACIA.

Several examples are given to illustrate Sacrobosco's text, but no new methods are introduced. In the matter of proofs, however, Dacia uses the check by nines as well as the subtraction of one number from the sum.

XXVI. LEWI BEN GERSON.

Process: The process begins at the right and is that in use at the present time. The sum is written below, and separated from the addends by a line, they being also separated from one another by lines.

Example:

```
  209
 ─────
 3089
 ─────
 7639
 ─────
10937
```

XXVIII. PLANUDES.

Def. Addition is uniting two or more numbers to form one sum.

Process: Begin at the right. Place the sum above. When more than nine arises from the addition of the digits in any order, hold the excess *in the mind*, and add it to the sum of the digits of the next higher order. (Cf. XVI.)

Example:

8030	2
5687	8
2343	3

Here the numbers at the right of the vertical line are used in the proof.

Proof: Check by nines.

XXXII. ALGORISMUS PROSAYCUS.

Def. Addition is the combining of a number or numbers with a number, so that the sum shall be known.

Term. tech.: *Addicio, addere; numerus cui debet fieri addicio; numerus addendus.*

Process: Begin at the right. Replace the upper number by the sum.

Example: 5782
6543.

Proof: By subtraction.

XXXIII. BELDAMANDI.

Def. Addition is uniting a number with a number, or numbers, to see what results.

Term. tech.: *additio, agregatio, summa totius illius agregationis.*

Process: Exactly like that used at the present time.

Example:		
	4123 2314 1431 2131 9999	to illustrate the case where the sum of the digits of any order is never greater than 9.
	2753 4968 8248 4031 20000	to illustrate the case where the sum is an article.
	9573 8164 4710 2937 25394	to illustrate the case where the sum is greater than 10.[1]

Proof: Check by nines, casting out nines from the columns, instead of from the rows.

[1] The error in the sum is found in the text.

XXXIV. KILLINGWORTH.

Term. tech.: *addere, addicio, aggregatum, productum.*

Process: Begin at the right. Place the sum above.

Example: Two illustrative examples are given, in each of which the sum is placed below, contrary to the directions given in the text.

4226 proba 5 } aggregat
 152 proba 8 } probarum 4
4376 proba 4

Proof: In a separate chapter the checks by nines and by sevens are given for all the operations.[1]

XXXV. A FIFTEENTH CENTURY ALGORISM.

In the analysis published, it is stated only that the checks by nines and by sevens are used.

XXXVI. A GERMAN ALGORISM.

Def. Addition is uniting one number to another.

Term. tech.: *additio.*

Process: Begin at the right. Replace the upper number by the sum.

Example: Several illustrative examples are given, among them 43000
 60543

Proof: By subtraction.

XXXVII. AL-KALCADI.

Def. Addition is the process of collecting numbers, one to others, so as to express them as a single sum.

Process: Write the numbers in rows, draw a line above and write the sum above the line.

[1] For the information concerning the Killingworth arithmetic I am indebted to Professor L. C. Karpinski who has made a study of the work.

Example: 115344

68765
46579

Note: The text directs that after adding 9 and 5, 1 shall be written below the 7 and added to 7 and 6, but the example is not so printed.

XXXVIII. PEURBACH.

Term. tech.: *addere, additio.*

Process: Like XXXIII. Several numbers are added. Peurbach says "*In unum addere numeros plures.*"

Proof: Check by nines.

SECTION VI.

Subtraction.

As is natural in a system developed where an abacus or a sand table is employed for numerical calculation, subtraction as taught in the earliest treatises, begins either at the right or at the left. The operation is defined as the process of taking away a smaller number from a greater, and the result after this subtraction usually replaces the minuend exactly as if counters had been used, and actually removed from the board. Later, when calculation with pen and paper became more common, the process began preferably at the right, and the remainder was written in a third line. Abraham ben Esra and Lewi ben Gerson write the remainder below the other numbers, but with these exceptions it was written above until in the work of Beldamandi (1410) we find it below, and separated from minuend and subtrahend by a horizontal line exactly as is the custom today.

In the earliest Latin works, in case a digit of the subtrahend is greater than the corresponding digit of the minuend, it is invariably the custom to borrow one from the next higher order of the minuend. The method of adding ten to the digit of the minuend, and one to the digit of next higher order in the subtrahend seems to have been introduced into Europe by Leonard of Pisa. We find it in the *Talkhys* of Al-Banna, but apparently it was not in common use in Europe until the 14th century, after which its popularity increased until in the 16th century, it was one of the most common methods of dealing with this case.[1] Of all the treatises examined, only the *Talkhys* gives any method other than the two above. Both the check by nines and that by the reverse operation of addition are used, and frequently both appear in the same work. The checks by sevens and by eights are found in the work of Al-Banna, and that by sevens in the 15th century algorism described by E. Rath.

[1] *Jackson. Sixteenth Century Arith.* p. 51

II. ALGORITMI DE NUMERO INDORUM.

Term. tech.: *minuere, diminutio; numerus inferior; remanencium figura.*

Process: Place units under units, tens under tens, etc. Begin at the left, subtract each digit of the subtrahend from the corresponding digit in the minuend, and write the remainder (*quod remanserit*) in the place of the digit of the minuend. When the digit of the subtrahend is greater than that of the minuend, borrow one from the next higher order in the minuend.

There are three kinds of subtraçtion.

(1) Where each digit of the subtrahend is less than the corresponding digit of the minuend.

(2) Where the remainder contains zeros.

(3) Is not given, possibly was the case in which some digit of the subtrahend is greater than the corresponding digit of the minuend.

Examples: All given in words.

6422 3211	to illustrate case (1)
1144 144	to illustrate case (2)

No proof.

III. MAHAVIRACARYA.

The eighth operation called *vyutkalita* discusses the subtraction of a part of a series from the whole.

V. SRIDHARACARYA.

Subtraction of a part of a series from the whole.

VI. AL-NASAWI.

In his analysis, Woepcke states only that Al-Nasawi uses the check by nines.

VII. AVICENNA.

2165 is given, but it is probable that the manuscript does
1321 not contain the example in this form.
844

IX. AL-HASSAR.

In the analysis, Suter states only that the process begins at the left.

X. BHASKARA.

See section on addition.

XI. LIBER ALGORISMI.

Def. To subtract is to take a number from a greater number.

Term. tech.: *diminuere, minuere, subtrahere; minuendus, major numerus, superior numerus; minuens, minor numerus, inferior numerus; residuus numerus.*

Process: Begin at the left. Borrow from next higher order of the minuend. Write the remainder in place of the minuend. There are three cases.

(1) Where no zeros occur in the remainder.

(2) Where one or more zeros occur in the remainder.

(3) Where it is not possible to borrow from the next higher order of the minuend.

Examples: 12025 to illustrate case (1)
3604

2444 to illustrate case (2)
144

10000 to illustrate case (3).
15

Proof: By addition, or check by nines.

XII. A TWELFTH CENTURY ALGORISM.

Term. tech: *diminutio, minuere, auferre; major; minor.*

Process: Begin at the right. Borrow from next higher order of the minuend. Position of remainder is not stated.

No example and no proof.

XIV. ABRAHAM BEN ESRA.

Process: Begin at the left. Borrow from the next higher order in the minuend. Write the remainder below.

Example:	5432	20
	2379	17
	3053	03

Proof: Check by nines.

XV. DEMONSTRATIO JORDANI DE ALGORISMO.

Def. To subtract is to find the excess of a greater over a smaller number.

Term. tech.:[1] *detrahere, detractio; major numerus; residuum.*

Process: The analysis states that the operation is carried out in the "*usual way,*" and that the method of borrowing is like that of XI. There are no illustrative examples.

Proof: By addition.

XVI. LEONARD OF PISA.

Term. tech.: *extractio, extrahere; major numerus; minor numerus; residuum.*

Process: Begin at the right. Place the remainder above. In case a digit of the minuend is less than the corresponding digit of the subtrahend, add ten to the upper number, subtract, and hold one in the hand. Add this one to the next figure of the subtrahend and proceed.

[1] Copied from Enestrom's article.

Example: Eight examples are given, among them

53337
81728
28391

Proof: Check by nines.

XVII. ALEXANDER DE VILLA DEI.

Term. tech.: *demere, subtrahere, subtractio; major numerus; minor numerus.*

Process: Explained in 15 lines. Begin at the right. If a digit of subtrahend is greater than a corresponding digit of minuend, borrow one from the digit of next higher order in the minuend. The remainder is to be written above. No mention is made of erasure.

No example is given.

Proof: By addition.

XVIII. SACROBOSCO.

Def. In subtraction it is proposed to find the excess of a greater over a smaller number, or

Subtraction is the taking away of one number from another in order to find the remainder.

Term. tech.: *subtractio, subtrahere; numerus a quo debet fiere subtractio; numerus subtrahendus; summa.*

Process: It is impossible to subtract a greater from a less number. The greater number is that which has the greater number of digits, or in case the number of digits is the same, it is that number in which the digit at the left is the greater.

Begin to subtract at the right or the left (preferably at the left). The remainder replaces the upper number. Borrow from the next higher order of the minuend. No example given.

Proof: By addition.

XIX. SALEM CODEX.

Term. tech.: *subtrahere, subtractio.*

Process: Begin at the right. Replace the upper number by the remainder. Borrow from the next higher order in the minuend.

Example:	810	The result is	666
	144		144

Proof: By addition.

XX. AL-BANNA.

Def. Subtraction is seeking what remains after rejecting one of two numbers from the other.

Process: There are two cases:

(1) Subtraction of the less from the greater. Begin at the right or left, preferably at the left. If a digit of the subtrahend is greater than the corresponding digit of the minuend

(a) Subtract the digit of the minuend from that of the subtrahend, and write the complement of the result, or

(b) Add ten to the digit of the minuend, subtract and carry one to the next higher digit of the subtrahend.

(2) Continued subtraction of the less from the greater until the remainder is less than the smaller number.[1]

No example is given.

Proof: Check by nines, eights, or sevens.

XXII. ALGORITHMUS DEMONSTRATUS.

Def. Subtraction of a number from a number is to diminish one by the other.

Term. tech.: *subtractio, subtrahere, detrahere; numerus superior, numerus major; numerus inferior, numerus minor, subtrahendus.*

[1] To facilitate the checks by 9's, 8's, and 7's.

Process: Begin at the right. The remainder replaces the upper number. Borrow from the next higher order of the minuend.

Example:
$$\begin{array}{cccccc} \underline{d} & \underline{o} & \underline{b} & \underline{a} & \underline{o} & \underline{o} \\ \underline{k} & \underline{h} & \underline{g} & \underline{f} & \underline{o} & \underline{o} \end{array}$$

Here, $a > f$, and $a - f = t$.

$b < g$ which necessitates borrowing from d. If $d - 1 = c$, and $(10 + b) - g = y$, the problem before subtracting h would stand.
$$\begin{array}{cccccc} \underline{c} & \underline{9} & \underline{y} & \underline{t} & \underline{o} & \underline{o} \\ \underline{k} & \underline{h} & \underline{g} & \underline{f} & \underline{o} & \underline{o} \end{array}$$

Proof: By addition.

XXIV. A THIRTEENTH CENTURY ALGORISM.

Def. To subtract is to take away a smaller from a greater number.

Term. tech.: *diminuere, diminutio; numerus major; numerus minor.*

Process: Begin at the right. Replace the upper number by the remainder. Borrow from the next higher order of the minuend.

Examples:
$$\begin{array}{r} 237 \\ 46 \end{array} \qquad \begin{array}{r} 1000000 \\ 999999 \end{array}$$

Proof: By addition.

XXV. PETRUS DE DACIA.

Three examples are given to illustrate Sacrobosco's text, but no new methods are introduced. Among the examples is
$$\begin{array}{r} 10222 \\ 5432 \end{array}$$

To determine which of the two numbers is the greater, the writer calls attention to the fact that it is sometimes necessary to consider figures other than those at the right, i. e., in 983 and 973. He also uses the check by nines as well as that of the reverse operation.

XXVI. LEWI BEN GERSON.

Process: Begin at the right. If a digit of the subtrahend is greater than the corresponding digit of the minuend, borrow one from the digit of next higher order in the minuend.

Example: In the example the numbers at the right of the vertical line are sexagesimal fractions. The remainder is written below the lower horizontal line. Above the upper horizontal line are the auxiliary quantities resulting from the necessity of borrowing.

	0	10	7	9		45				
3	1	0	8	0	0	46	35	47	0	53
		2	0	6	50	0	37			
3	0	8	7	3	10	45	58	47	0	53

No proof.

XXVII. PLANUDES.

Def. Subtraction is the taking away of a number from another number, and seeing what is the result. A less may be taken from a greater or an equal from an equal, but to take a greater from a less is impossible, for what one has not cannot be taken away from him.

Process: The greater number is that which has the greater number of digits, or whose left hand digit is greater. (Cf. XVIII.)

Begin at the right. Place the remainder above. When a digit of the subtrahend is greater than that of the minuend

(1) Add ten to the minuend, and carry one to the next figure of the subtrahend, or

(2) Borrow from the next higher order of the minuend.

Example:

54612
18769
54612
35843
1111

To illustrate case (1). Here the minuend and subtrahend are below the line, and the remainder and proof above.

08984
24031
35142
26158

To illustrate case (2). Here 26158 is to be subtracted from 35142. The remainder is 8984, and 2, 4, 0, 3, are the remainders after 1 has been subtracted from each of the digits of the minuend.

Proof: By addition.

XXXII. ALGORISMUS PROSAYCUS.

Def. Subtraction is taking away a number, or numbers, from a number.

Term. tech.: *Subtraccio; numerus subtrahendus; numerus a quo fit subtraccio; numerus remanens.*

Process: The subtrahend must be less than, or equal to the minuend. Begin at the right. Borrow from the next higher order in the minuend. Replace the minuend by the remainder.

Example: 140321
46523

Proof: By addition.

XXXIII. BELDAMANDI.

Def. Subtraction is taking away a number from a number to see what remains.

Term. tech.: *subtrahere, subtractio; numerus a quo debet fiere subtractio; numerus subtrahendus; numerus qui remanet.*

Process: Begin at the right. Borrow from next higher order in the minuend. Write the result below under a line (*virgula*).

Example: 50073
36582
―――
13491

Proof: Check by nines. Beldamandi calls attention to Sacrobosco's check by reversing the operation.

XXXIV. KILLINGWORTH.

Term. tech.: *subtrahere, subtractio; numerus remanens.*

Process: Begin at the right. When a digit of the minuend is less than the corresponding digit of the subtrahend, add ten to it, and carry one to the next digit of the subtrahend. The text directs that the remainder shall be written above, but in the illustrative problems, it is written below.

XXXV. A FIFTEENTH CENTURY ALGORISM.

The analysis states that in case the digit of the minuend is less than that of the subtrahend, it is necessary to increase it by ten and carry one to the next figure of the subtrahend.

Proof: By addition, or check by sevens.

XXXVI. A GERMAN ALGORISM.

Def. Subtraction is taking a smaller number from a greater.

Term. tech.: *Subtracio; die minsten numerus; die mesten numerus, oversten orden.*

Process: Begin at the right. Borrow from the next higher order of the minuend. It is not stated whether the remainder is written above or below.

Proof: By addition.

XXXVII. AL-KALCADI.

Def. Subtraction is to know the excess of one number over another.

Process: Begin at the right. Draw a line above the numbers and place the remainder above the line. When the digit of the minuend is less than that of the subtrahend, increase it by ten and carry one to the next figure of the subtrahend.

Example:

$$\begin{array}{r} 2102 \\ \hline 9726 \\ 7624 \end{array}$$

No proof is given.

XXXVIII. PEURBACH.

Term. tech.: *subtrahere, subtractio; numerus a quo debet fiere subtractio; subtrahendus.*

Process: Begin at the right. Borrow from the digit of next higher order in the minuend. Write the result below, separated from the other numbers by a line. No example is given.

Proof: Check by nines.

SECTION VII.

Mediation and Duplation.

Mediation and duplation are characteristic of that class of arithmetics which may rightly be called *algorisms*. They do not appear in the Hindu works, in the Arabic treatises which were written independently of Al-Khowarizmi, nor in the *Liber abaci*, but are found almost invariably in the other Latin algorisms, and in those of the vernacular following the same model.

Cantor thinks that the introduction of duplation is due to Egyptian influence acting through Greek channels,[1] but there is no evidence to support this theory other than that the Egyptian multiplication was a combination of doubling and adding. The *Liber algorismi de pratica arismetrice*, supposed to be based upon the work of Al-Khowarizmi, at least in the first part, states that these operations were introduced because of their importance in the extraction of roots,[2] and it is possible that some such idea may have influenced Al-Khowarismi.

Sacrobosco considers duplation a species of addition, and the fact that so many later works give the same definition is one of the many evidences of the great influence exerted by the *Algorismus vulgaris* upon the arithmetics of this period. In the earlier treatises mediation begins at the right, and duplation at the left, showing the influence of the abacus reckoning, but the inconvenience of this method when pen and paper are used was recognized before the end of the period under consideration.

[1] *Vorlesungen I p. 674, ed. 1894.*

[2] *"Nota quia duplare, et mediare . . . sub scientia multiplicandi et diuidendi continetur. Dimidiare etenim est species diuidendi, et duplare species multiplicandi; et tamen quia necessaria sunt ad inueniendam radicem, que duplando et mediando inuenitur. Ideo hic per se ponuntur, cum tamen post tractatum multiplicandi, et diuidendi deberent conuenientius poni." p. 33.*

II. ALGORITMI DE NUMERO INDORUM.

Mediation precedes duplation.

Term. tech.: *mediare; duplare.*

Process: Mediation begins at the right. Take half of each digit. If the last digit is uneven, take half of the digit next smaller, call the half of the one remaining, thirty sixtieths, and write it under the result.[1] If any other digit is uneven, take half of the digit next smaller, but add five to the digit which stands at the right.

To double, begin at the left and double each digit.

No examples are given.

Proof: Check by nines.

VI. AL-NASAWI.

That Al-Nasawi considered mediation and duplation as separate operations though of somewhat different character from the others is shown by the arrangement of the chapters. (Cf. Section III, VI.)

IX. AL-HASSAR.

Mediation precedes duplation.

Begin at the left.

XI. LIBER ALGORISMI.

Duplation precedes mediation.

Def. To double a number is to collect the sum when doubled.

To halve a number is to divide it into two equal parts.

Term. tech.: *duplare; mediare, demidiare.*

Process: Both mediation and duplation are performed as in II. The treatise states that the result replaces the original number which is erased.

[1] *Scita quod fraciones appellentur multis nominibus in numerabilibus, atque, infinitis, ut medietas, tercia, quarta, nona et decima, et una pars ex. XIII., et pars ex. X. VIII. et cetera. Set indi posuerunt exitum partium suarum ex sexaginta; diuiserunt enim unum in . LX. partes quas nominauerunt minuta. p. 17.* Both sexagesimal and common fractions are found in Hindu works.

Example: To double 978. result | 1956 |

To halve 9783. Process	Process	Result	Result
	55		4891
	9783		30
	4341		
	30		

which is the author's method of writing 4891 $\frac{30}{60}$

Proof: For duplation, divide by two, or check by nines.
For mediation, double the result.

XII. A TWELFTH CENTURY ALGORISM.

Mediation precedes duplation.

Term. tech.: *mediatio; duplicatio.*

Process: Mediation performed as in II.
To double, add a number to itself. (Cf. XVIII.)

No examples are given.

Proof: In case of duplation, check by nines.

XV. DEMONSTRATIO JORDANI DE ALGORISMO.

Duplation precedes mediation.

Def. Duplation is the process of finding the double of a number.

Mediation is the process of finding half of an even number, or of an odd number minus one.

Term. tech: *duplare; dimidiare.*

Process: Begin to double at the left, to halve at the right. The remainder is expressed as a half.

No example is given.

XVII. ALEXANDER DE VILLA DEI.

Duplation precedes mediation.

Term. tech.: *duplare; mediare.*

Process: Lines 30 and 31 are as follows.

Subtrahis aut addis a dextris vel mediabis;
A leva dupla, divide, multiplicaque.

In line 68 we are told to begin to double with the *first* figure. Up to this point, *prima figura* has always indicated the digit at the right, though in the work on division it indicates that on the left. No mention of erasure is made.

To halve, begin at the right, and replace each number by its half. If the units digit is uneven, subtract one before halving. If any other digit is uneven, subtract one before halving and add 5 to the half of the preceding digit.

No examples are given. Prove mediation by doubling.

XVIII. SACROBOSCO.

Mediation precedes duplation.

Def. Mediation is the process of finding half of a number.
Duplation is the process of finding the sum of a number added to itself.

Term. tech.: *mediatio, mediare, numerus mediandus; duplatio, duplare.*

Process: Mediation like XI. In case of an uneven number, we may write either thirty sixtieths or δ which is a symbol for $\frac{1}{2}$.
Duplation like XI. The statement is made that it is possible but not convenient, to begin at the right. No examples are given.

Proof: Reverse operation in each case.

Note: It is in the section on duplation that the quotation from the *Carmen de algorismo* is given.

Subtrahis aut addis a dextris aut mediabis,
A laeva dupla, divide multiplicaque,
Extrahe redicem duplam sub parte sinistra.

XIX. SALEM CODEX.

Duplation and mediation treated together.

Term. tech.: *dupplatio, dupplare; demidiatio, dedupplatio, demidiare.*

Process: To double, write the number under itself and add. Begin at the right. Replace the upper number by the sum.

No explanation is given for the process of mediation.

Example: To double 532. Result 1064
532.

Proof: Subtract 532 from 1064.

XXII. ALGORITHMUS DEMONSTRATUS.

Duplation precedes mediation.

Def. To double a number is to take its sum twice.
Mediation is to leave half of a number.

Term. tech.: *duplare, duplacio; dimidiare.*

Process: In duplation begin at the left.

In the case of mediation, it is stated that since it is impossible to take half of an odd number, in such a case, we find half of the number next smaller. Begin at the right. In both processes, the result replaces the original number.

Proof: By the reverse operations.

XXV. PETRUS DE DACIA.

Mediation precedes duplation.

The commentary follows Sacrobosco's text and illustrates each step of the process. The custom of writing thirty sixtieths rather than one half, he calls "*more astronomorum.*" He gives the example 510321, and in the process, uses the symbol δ, but writes the final result. 255160 *et unum dimidium.*

As an illustration of the process of duplation, Dacia doubles the result of his mediation to get 510321.

Prove by reverse operations, or by casting out nines.

XXXII. ALGORITHMUS PROSAYCUS.

Mediation precedes duplation.

Def. Mediation is finding half of a number.
Duplation is doubling a number.[1]

[1] Triplation (*triplicacio*) and quadruplation (*quadruplacio*) are mentioned also.

Term. tech.: *Mediacio, mediare; duplacio, duplare.*

Process: Mediation begins at the right. If the number is uneven the remainder is indicated by a *d* signifying dimidius.

Duplation begins at the left.

Example: Halving 610541 gives 305270. Doubling 54608 gives 109216.

No proofs.

XXXIII. BELDAMANDI.

Mediation precedes duplation.

Def. Mediation is the process of finding half of a number.

Duplation is the process of adding a number to itself.

Term. tech.: *mediare, mediatio; duplare, duplatio.*

Process: In mediation, draw a line below the given number. Begin at the left. If a digit is even write its half below it, if odd write half of the next smaller number, and add five to half the next digit to the right. If the units digit is odd, place the sign for one half after the result, or

In case any digit is uneven, take half of the number next smaller and add ten to the digit at its right, before dividing by two.

In duplation, draw a line below. Begin at the right and double each digit.

Example: $\frac{9080753}{4540376\frac{1}{2}}$; $\frac{540603}{1081206}$.

Proof: Check by nines.

Note: Beldamandi calls attention to the fact that Sacrobosco proves his results by reversing the operations.

XXXIV. KILLINGWORTH.

Duplation precedes mediation.

Term. tech.: *duplicatio, duplare, duplatio, mediacio, mediare, mediatio.*

Process: Both mediation and duplation begin at the right. In mediation, the number of figures used is reduced by noting whether the next figure at the left of that upon which the operation is being performed is odd or even. If odd, add 5 at once to the result of the mediation. The text states that the result is to be placed above, but in the illustrative examples it is written below. Similarly, the text directs that the result of duplation shall be written above and the numbers carried written below, but the problems given are in modern form without the dividing line.

XXXV. A FIFTEENTH CENTURY ALGORISM.

Mediation appears as a special case of division, and not as a separate operation. There is no mention of duplation.

XXXVI. A GERMAN ALGORISM.

Duplation precedes mediation.

Term. tech.: *duplicacio; mediacio.*

Process: Begin to double at the left. The result replaces the original number.

Begin mediation at the right. If the number is uneven, subtract one, and make a sign to show that one has been subtracted, for it is impossible to take half of one. No examples or proofs are given.

XXXVII. PEURBACH.

Mediation precedes duplation.

Term. tech.: *demidiare, mediatio; duplare, duplatio.*

Process: Begin to halve at the left. If a digit is odd, subtract one, and add ten to the next digit at the right. If the units digit is odd, subtract one, and write $\frac{1}{2}$ after the result. Prove by adding the result to itself, or check by nines.

To double, write the number under itself and add. Prove by halving, or check by nines.

SECTION VIII.

Multiplication.

The works of this period, in their treatment of the subject of multiplication are full of interest, for we find in them not only all of the eight methods given by Pacciuolo, but also many ingenious devices for the multiplication of particular numbers.

Though the character of the Hindu works makes their interpretation somewhat difficult, it is possible to distinguish several methods. *Capátá-sand'hi* is probably the method adopted by Al-Khowarizmi. Though the process of operation is not made clear, Māhāvira and Sridhāra tell us to write the factors "*in the manner of the leaves of a door*" which suggests the arrangement as given in the translation of the Arabic treatise, as the repetition of the multiplier suggests the method of operation. *Talst'ha* is evidently a form of cross multiplication.. According to Ganesa, a 16th century commentator,[1] the process is exactly that given in the *Liber abaci*, but neither in the Hindu nor the Arabic works examined has there been found any more definite statement than "*multiply each digit of the multiplier by each digit of the multiplicand, according to their orders.*" Multiplication by parts includes two divisions, *subdivision of form* and *separation of digits*, the former referring to the subdivision of the multiplier into factors or into integrant parts, and the latter being explained in various ways by different commentators. To these three methods Bhaskara adds two others which are simply modifications of the rule for multiplication by integrant parts, in which one of the parts chosen is an article. Complementary multiplication as shown by the formula $ab = 10a - (10 - b)a$, might be a form of this method.

The Arabic treatises are remarkable for the many devices used in multiplication. Their writers seem to have grasped

[1] Colebrooke, p. 6 note.

much more clearly than did the Europeans of the same period, the possibilities of the decimal notation, and many rules which are considered algebraic at the present time appear in their works on arithmetic.

The *Liber abaci*, as its author states, is largely a compendium of Hindu methods.[1] Though cross multiplication is found in nearly every Hindu or Arabic treatise, the *lightning method* given by Leonard in which the partial products are held *in the hand* or *in the heart* does not appear in them, and it is possible that this expedient may have been added by him.

The advance made by the other Latin algorists is chiefly a matter of arrangement. Unless we admit the possible exception of complementary multiplication, there is no method in these works that had not already appeared in Hindu or Arabic texts; but whereas these were usually a disconnected mass of rules and examples, the Latin works are often written with pedagogical clearness and precision. The process of multiplication as described by Al-Khowarizmi, though showing slight variations in the different works, is found almost universally, and that Al-Karkhi is responsible for many of the methods used, is clear upon comparison of the *Liber algorismi* with the *Kâfi fîl Hisâb.* Complementary multiplication as applied to numbers less than ten, is not found in the oriental works, but the case in which the complement is the difference between the number and the next article is not uncommon. The fact that complementary multiplication does appear in the earliest works, which are avowedly translations, seems to point to an Arabic origin, but Leonard of Pisa does not introduce it into the *Liber abaci,* as would have been natural if it had been common among the Arabs. If the *Talchis* of Al-Banna written about half a century later does contain an example of it, the question arises as to why the general rule was not introduced into the arithmetic of Al-Kalçadi. It is evident that a decision of the question must await the study of other Arabic works.

[1] *Quare amplectens stricuius ipsum modum indorum, et attentius studens in eo, ex proprio sensu quedam addens . . . summam huius libri . . . componere laboraui.*

I. BRAHMAGUPTA.

Process: (1) "The multiplicand is repeated like a string for cattle, as often as there are integrant parts in the multiplier, and is severally multiplied by them, and the products are added together."

(2) The multiplicand is multiplied as many times as there are parts in the multiplier.

Example: None is given by Brahmagupta, but his commentator Chaturveda gives the multiplication of 235 by 288 as follows

(1)	235	2	270	which added make 67680.
	235	8	1880	
	235	8	1880	

(2) multiplication by parts.

(a)	235	9	2115	which added make 67680.
	235	8	1880	
	235	151	35485	
	235	120	28200	

(b) 235 by 9 is 2115
2115 by 8 is 16920
16920 by 4 is 67680

Chaturveda adds "The method by parts is taught by Scandasena and others. In like manner the other methods of multiplication, as *tat-st'ha*[1] and *capata-sand'hi*,[2] taught by the same authors, may be inferred by the student's own ingenuity."

II. ALGORITMI DE NUMERO INDORUM.

Def. In multiplication it is necessary to double one number as many times as there are units in the other.[3]

[1] Cross multiplication.

[2] The method of Al-Khowarizmi.

[3] The use of the word *double* in this sense is Arabic It is not found in Hindu works.

Term. tech.: *multiplicare, multiplicatio; numerus superior; numerus inferior.* The product is designated by the expression *figura numeri, qui exiuit nobis de multiplicatione.*

Process: First know how to multiply digits by digits. Then write one number on a tablet, or anywhere else you choose (*in tabula, vel in qualibet re alia quam volueris*) and write the second number under it so that the first digit of the lower number shall be under the last digit of the other. Begin at the left and multiply each digit of the lower number by the last of the upper, writing each result above the corresponding number of the lower. Move the lower number one place to the right, and multiply each digit by that digit of the upper number which is above the first digit of the lower number. Move the lower number to the right and proceed as before.

But if at any time the first digit of the lower number is below a zero, move it one place to the right, since zero multiplied by any number is nothing. And when the lower number has been moved to the right and has been multiplied by a digit of the upper number add the product resulting from this multiplication to whatever may have been written above.

Example: To multiply *duo milia tercentos. XXVI. in. CCXIIII.*[or]

The process is as shown in Fig. 1. Here the figures in heavy type form the product. All the figures of the partial products have been erased in the course of the multiplication, and the product should stand in a line above the multiplicand.

Proof: Check by nines.

7
6**7**
926**6**
8144
42828**4**
2326
214
214
214

Fig. 1.

III. MAHAVIRACARYA.

1998
27

2×1	2				
2×9	1	8			
2×9		1	8		
2×8			1	6	
7×1		7			
7×9		6	3		
7×9			6	3	
7×8				5	6
	5	3	9	4	6

FIG. 2.

Process: Place the multiplicand and the multiplier in the manner of the hinges of a door. Multiply the multiplicand by the multiplier in accordance with the normal, or the reverse method. In a note by the translator the normal method is said to be the same as I.(2)(b) and the reverse method is illustrated as in Fig. 2. The "*hinges of a door*" suggests an arrangement like that of Al-Khowarizmi.

Example: Sixteen examples without solutions are given. The first is as follows. *Lotuses were given away in offering, eight of them to each Jina temple. How many were given away to 144 temples?*

V. SRIDHARACARYA.

Process: (1) Place the multiplicand below the multiplier as in the junction of the leaves of a door.[1] Multiply in order, directly or inversely repeating the multiplier each time.[2] This method is called *kapadasandhi*.

(2) "Another method is called *tatstha* because the multiplier stands still therein."[3]

(3) Multiplication by parts.

(a) Subdivision of form.[4]

(b) Separation of digits.[5]

No examples are given.

[1] Cf. III.

[2] Note that the factor to be repeated is here placed *above* the other.

[3] Cross multiplication. Cf. Colebrook's translation of the *Lilavati*, p. 6 note.

[4] This includes I (2) (a) and (b).

[5] Cf. I. 1.

VI. AL-NASAWI.

Woepcke states that Chapter III. contains the definition of multiplication and a description of the kinds of multiplication and of the process in the case of integers, but this is not translated. In a note it is stated that the example in Fig. 3 is given by Al-Nasawi, who ascribes the method to the Hindus. The problem is to multiply 324 by 753. Here all figures except those in heavy type are to be erased in the course of the operation, and replaced by those above them. To prove, he uses the check by nines.

43
309
2977
215962
324
753
753
753

FIG. 3.

VII. AVICENNA.

275
122
———
550
550
275
———
33550

FIG. 4.

In the translation, the example in Fig. 4 is given to illustrate the check by nines, but probably it is not found in this form in the manuscript. I have not seen the same arrangement in any work earlier than that of Beldamandi (1410).

VIII. AL-KARKHI.

Def. For those who do not admit the division of unity: Multiplication is the process of taking one of the factors as many times as there are units in the other.

For whose who admit the division of unity: Multiplication is the process of finding a number to which one of the factors is related, as unity is to the other.[1]

Process:[2] (1) To multiply *simple numbers* (numbers containing one significant figure): Neglect the thousands, mul-

[1] Cf. Euclid VII. def. 15.
[2] No figures are used in the text.

tiply the remaining numbers, and annex the thousands. Ex. 200,000,000 by 30,000.:200× 30=6000. Since tens by hundreds gives thousands, the result is 6,000,000,000,000.

(2) To multiply *compound numbers* (numbers containing two or more significant figures): Multiply each digit of the multiplier by each digit of the multiplicand, beginning at the left. Add the results. The example given is 555 by 444. The process would be carried out as in Fig. 5. Al-Karkhi states that nine multiplications will be required since each factor is of the third order.

500×400=	200000
500× 40=	20000
500× 4=	2000
50×400=	20000
50× 40=	2000
50× 4=	200
5×400=	2000
5× 40=	200
5× 4=	20
	246420

FIG. 5.

(3) (a) Find the ratio of one factor to some *simple number*, multiply the other factor by this ratio, and give to the result the order of the simple number chosen. Ex. 125×84 ; 125 is $\frac{1}{8}$ of 1000 ; $\frac{1}{8}$ of $84=10\frac{1}{2}$; therefore the result is 10500.

(b) If there is no convenient ratio, first add (or subtract) an arbitrary number. Find the ratio of the sum (or difference) to some simple number and proceed as in (a). Then multiply the number added (or subtracted), by the unaltered factor, and subtract (or add) the result. Ex. 123×252; (123+2) is $\frac{1}{8}$ of 1000; $\frac{1}{8}$ of $252=31\frac{1}{2}$, therefore the result is 31500−2×252=30996.

(c) In case one factor is such a number as $12833\frac{1}{3}$, break it into 12500 and $333\frac{1}{3}$. Say 12500 is $\frac{1}{8}$ of 100000, and $333\frac{1}{3}$ is $\frac{1}{3}$ of 1000 and proceed as above.

(4) Application of (3) to both factors. Ex. 2500 × 750 : $\frac{2500}{1000}=2\frac{1}{2}$; $\frac{750}{100}=7\frac{1}{2}$. $2\frac{1}{2}\times 7\frac{1}{2}=18\frac{1}{2}.\frac{1}{4}$ therefore the result is 1875000.

(5) From the square of half the sum take the square of half the difference. This rule is the best when the sum is a simple number. No example is given.

(6) (a) A rule which may be expressed symbolically as follows $(10a+b)(10c+d)=[c(10a+b)+da]10+bd$. Ex. To multiply 44 by 33, the process is $44\times3=132$; $132+3\times4=144$. $10\times144=1440$; $1440+3\times4=1452$.

(b) $(10a+b)(10a+c)=(10a+b+c)a.10+bc$. Ex. 83×83; $83+3=86$; $86\times8=688$. $6880+9=6889$.

(7) $(10a\pm b)(10a-c)=100a^2\pm10ab-10ac\mp bc$. Ex. $53\times48=(50+3)(50-2)=2500+50\times3-50+2-2\times3=2444$. . $98\times97=(100-2)(100-3)$.

(8) $ab=a^2\times\frac{b}{a}$. Ex. $25\times35=25^2\times1\frac{11}{25}$.[1]

Proof: Check by nines.

IX. AL-HASSAR.

Process: The chapter on multiplication is divided into ten parts, in which are multiplied together numbers of one digit by numbers of one digit, numbers of two digits by numbers of one digit, etc. In the tenth subdivision is given the multiplication of 43 by 76, after the method of II. Figures are erased in the process of multiplication, the final result appearing in the line above the upper numbers.

X. BHASKARA.

Process: (1) Multiply the multiplicand by each digit of the multiplier beginning at the left, the multiplier being repeated.

(2) Subdivision of form

(a) Like I, (2)(a) ex: $135\times12=135\times8+135\times4$.

(b) Like I, (2)(b) ex: $135\times12=135\times3\times4$.

[1] The fraction is given as $\frac{2}{5}+\frac{1}{5}\times\frac{1}{5}$.

(3) Like I, 1. Example

135	1	135
135	2	270
		1620.

(4 & 5) Multiply the multiplicand by the multiplier diminished (or increased) by an arbitrary quantity, and add (or subtract) the product of the multiplicand by the assumed quantity. Example: $135\times 12=135\times 10+135\times 2.$; $135\times 12=135\times 20-135\times 8.$

Example: Beautiful and dear Lilavati, whose eyes are like a fawn's! tell me what are the numbers resulting from one hundred and thirty five, taken into twelve? If thou be skilled in multiplication by whole or by parts whether by subdivision of form or separation of digits.

XI. LIBER ALGORISMI.

Def. To multiply a number is to count it as many times as there are units in itself or in another number. For a number may be multiplied by itself or by another.

Term. tech.: *multiplicare, multiplicatio; numerus multiplicandus, numerus superior; numerus multiplicans, numerus inferior; summe ex multiplicatione, productus.*

Process: (1) (p. 38, 41.) The same as that of Al-Khawarizmi. The same emphasis is laid upon the necessity of being able to multiply digits, and the same discussion as to the use of the zero. The product is written in a line with the multiplicand, the digits being erased as others are found to take their places.

Example: 104 by 206. The example is as follows

104
206

the process is explained in words, and the result is written

214	24.

. As a proof the author gives the check by nines, though he realizes its inadequacy, for he says, "this rule will show when the multiplication is incorrect, but will not prove that it is right." He suggests also as a proof, the division of the product by either of the factors.

(2) (p. 97 under the heading. "*De multiplicatio digitorum in se.*)

(a) To multiply by itself a number less than ten; multiply it by ten (*deculpata*), and subtract the product of itself multiplied by the difference between itself and ten. i.e., $a^2 = 10a - a(10-a)$.

Example: $6\times6 = 6\times10 - 6\times4 = 36$.

(b) To multiply two unequal digits.

(i) Multiply the less by the difference between ten and the greater, and subtract the result from ten times the less. i.e., $ab = 10a - a(10-b)$; $a<b$.

Example: $5\times7 = 5\times10 - 3\times5 = 35$.

(ii) Multiply the greater by the difference between ten and the less, and subtract the result from ten times the greater ie $ab = 10b - b(10-a)$; $a<b$.

Example: $5\times7 = 7\times10 - 5\times7 = 35$.

(3) (p. 116–120.) To multiply articles by articles, digits by digits, or composites by composites, multiply figure by figure. In each case add the orders of the digits multiplied and subtract one, the result will show the order of the product.

(4) Find the ratio of one of the factors to its limit. Multiply this ratio by the other factor and by the limit.

Example: 25×32; $25 = \frac{1}{4}$ of 100; $\frac{1}{4}$ of $32 = 8$; $8\times100 = 800$.

(5) To multiply two numbers with the same articles but different digits; multiply the digits together and the articles together and add the results. Add the digits, multiply the sum by the article and add the result to the first product. i.e., $(10a+b)(10a+c) = 100a^2 + bc + 10a(b+c)$.

Example: 16×18: $6\times8 = 48$, $10\times10 = 100$, $100 + 48 = 148$.
$6+8 = 14$, $10\times14 = 140$, $140 + 148 = 288$.

(6) To multiply the square root of one number by the square root of another, multiply the numbers and take the square root of the product.

Example: $\sqrt{10}\times\sqrt{40}=\sqrt{10\times40}=\sqrt{400}=20$. "Moreover these numbers will proceed according to the rule of three."

(7) A repetition of (3) with two illustrations.

(a) 70 by 20. Say $7\times2=14$. Then since each is of the second order say $2+2-1=3$ $\therefore$ 1400 is the result.

(b) 23 by 64. In the margin is written $\begin{matrix}2 & & 3\\ & \times & \\ 6 & & 4\end{matrix}$ but no mention is made of the cross. A figure is given in which the sum is to be found by adding, and is 1472. The columns appearing in the figure are not mentioned in the text, and evidently are used only to emphasize the orders of the digits.

		1	2
	1	8	
1	2	8	

(8) To multiply numbers with one significant figure only, reject the thousands, and multiply, then add the number of iterations in each. A great number of examples are given of which the last is 50,000,000 by 300,000,000,000,000. $50\times300=150{,}000$ (an error in the text) add two and four, and repeat thousand six times.

XII. A TWELFTH CENTURY ALGORISM.

Term. tech.: *multiplicare, multiplicatione; multiplicandus, inferior numerus, multiplicans, multiplicator, superior numerus.*

Process: (1) Multiplication of digits. (1st species)

(a) a table up to 9×9, arranged in triangular form.

(b) subtract from the less number the difference between ten and the greater (*differentia majoris*), multiply the result by ten (*denominatione facere*) and add to the result the product of the differences between ten and each of the numbers. i.e., $ab=[b-(10-a)]10+(10-a)\ (10-b);\ a>b$.

(2) Multiplication of numbers with one significant figure. (2nd species) Like II.

Example: 10×10 and 40×300. The product takes the place of the upper number.

(3) Multiplication of other numbers (3rd species) Like II.

Example: 1024 by 306.

Proof: Check by nines.

XIV. ABRAHAM BEN ESRA.

Process: (1) To multiply multiples of ten, multiply the significant figures, add the orders and subtract one "for a base," to find the order of the result.[1]

(2) When one of the two factors exceeds an article by as much as the article exceeds the other, square the article and subtract the square of the difference ie, $(10a-b)(10a+b) = 100a^2 - b^2$.

Example:
$$29 \times 31 = 30^2 - 1^2$$
$$66 \times 54 = 60^2 - 6^2$$
$$250 \times 350 = 300^2 - 50^2.$$

(3) An "important method." (ben Esra's own discovery.)

(a) To square a number, square its third part, multiply by 10, and subtract the square of its third part.

Example: $3^2 = 1^2(10) - 1,^2$ i.e., $a^2 = \left(\frac{a}{3}\right)^2 10 - \left(\frac{a}{3}\right)^2$
$$15^2 = 5^2(10) - 5^2$$
$$24^2 = 8^2(10) - 8^2$$

(b) If the number is 1 more than a multiple of 3, subtract 1, and proceed as in (a), but add to the result the original number and the number less 1. i. e.

$$a^2 = \left(\frac{a-1}{3}\right)^2 10 - \left(\frac{a-1}{3}\right)^2 + (a-1) + a.$$

Example:
$$7^2 = (2)^2 10 - (2)^2 + 6 + 7.$$
$$22^2 = 7^2(10) - (7)^2 + 21 + 22.$$

[1] ben Ezra explains later (p. 88) that the numbers 1-9 are the true numbers representing the 9 circles, the multiples of these being related numbers of which tens should be the first, hundreds the second, etc., but that arithmeticians have put units for the first, tens for the second, etc., and therefore it is necessary to subtract one for a *base*. The *related numbers* date back to the time of Appollonius of Perga.

(c) If the number is 2 more than a multiple of 3. Add 1, and proceed as in (a), but subtract the original number, and the number plus 1. i.e., $a^2 = \left(\frac{a+1}{3}\right)^2 10 - \left(\frac{a+1}{3}\right)^2 - a - (a+1)$.

Example: $23^2 = (8^2)10 - 8^2 - 23 - 24$.

(4)—(a) Like VIII. (2)

Example: 13×28.

$$\begin{array}{r} 10 \times 20 \\ 10 \times \ 8 \\ 3 \times 20 \\ 3 \times \ 8 \end{array}$$

(b) Like VIII. 6 (b)

Example: $13 \times 16 = (10 + 3 + 6)10 + 3 \times 6$.

(c) When the factors have the same article and the sum of the digits is 10. i. e.,

$$(10a + b)\ (10a + \{10 - b\}) = 10(a + 1)10a + b(10 - b).$$

Example: $24 \times 26 = 10 \times 3 \times 20 + 4 \times 6$.

(5) To multiply any number by any other number. Write the smaller number above, although this is not necessary. Begin at the *right*, and multiply each digit of the lower number by the first digit of the upper and write the product *below*, in a third line. Then multiply the second number of the upper number by each of the lower numbers, and write the product below, beginning under the second digit of the upper number. Continue until the last digit of the upper number has been multiplied by the lower, and add the partial products.

$$\begin{array}{r} 127 \\ 355 \\ \hline 32335 \\ 115 \\ 61 \\ 55 \\ \hline 45085 \end{array}$$

FIG. 6.

Example: To multiply 127 by 355. The process is as shown in Fig. 6.

Proof: Check by nines.

XV. DEMONSTRATIO JORDANI DE ALGORISMO.

Def. To multiply is to find a number which will contain one of two numbers as many times as the other contains unity.

Term. tech.:[1] *multiplicare, multiplicatio; multiplicatus, numerus superior; multiplicans, numerus inferior; productus.*

Process: Same as XI. (1). No examples or proof.

XVI. LEONARD OF PISA.

Term. tech.: *multiplicare, multiplicatio; summe multiplicatione.*

The chapter on multiplication is preceded by an explanation of finger symbolism, and by tables for the addition and multiplication of integers, for the addition of articles up to 90+90, and for the multiplication of numbers up to 10×10, and of 10×20. It is divided into 8 parts of which 1–5 treat of the method of cross multiplication using a tablet (*scribantur in tabula dealbata in qua littere leuiter deleantur*, p. 7). Parts 6 and 7 discuss the same subject without the use of a tablet, and part 8 describes the quadrilateral method. Each of the parts concerned with cross multiplication contains a paragraph stating the order of the several multiplications and additions, followed by examples to illustrate the cases in which the factors are equal, that in which they are unequal, and that in which zeros occur in one or both factors.

If the numbers are unequal the greater is always written below with units under units, tens under tens, etc. There is no mention of erasure other than that in the description of the tablet, but the tens or hundreds digit is to be held in the hand (*in manu*) in the place of units or tens until it is added to the result of the next multiplication.

Process: Part 1. The multiplication of two figures by two figures, or of one figure by many.

[1] Copied from Eneström's article.

(a) Example: 12×12. In the margin, the solution is given as in Fig. 7. The process is as follows: the product of the units is 4, which is written above the units of the factors. Multiply units of the multiplier by tens of the multiplicand also units of the multiplicand by tens of the multiplier, add the products and write the result which is 4 above the tens of the factors. Multiply tens of the multiplicand by tens of the multiplier, add the products and write the result which is 1 in the place of hundreds. Other examples are 37×37 and 98×98.

descriptio	4
	12
prima	12
	44
secunda	12
	12
	144
ultima	12
	12

Fig. 7.

(b) To multiply 37×49; 7× 9
7×40
30× 9
30×40

(c) To multiply 49×8; or 308 by 7. Write the greater number below, and the product above the smaller number. Begin at the right and multiply each digit of the greater number by the smaller.

(d) To multiply 70×81. Remove the zero, multiply and annex the zero.

Part 2. To multiply three or two figures by three figures. The process is the *lightning method* of cross multiplication. Examples used for illustration are 345×345; 607×607; 780×780; 900×900; 370×451; 123×456. In all cases where the factors contain zeros at the right, these are removed before multiplication.

Part 3. Four or three or two figures by four figures. The examples are 1234×1234; 2345×6789; 5000×7000; 5100×3701, and the method used is that of cross multiplication.

Part 4. Five figures by five figures. The example is 12345 by 12345. The method used is cross multiplication.

Part 5. More than five figures. The example is 12345678 by 87654321. The method used is cross multiplication.

Part 6. Method without a tablet. Keep the numbers *in the heart* (*retineat descriptionem numerorum in corde quos multiplicare voluerit*), and in the process hold the product in the hand.

Example: 12×12; 48×48; 23 by 57.

The multiplication of 48×48 is given as follows: 8×8=64. Place 4 *in the left hand in the place of units*, and hold 6 *in the right hand in the place of hundreds.* 8×4+8×4=64 which added to the 6 in the right hand gives 70, of which place 0 *in the left hand in the place of tens*, and keep 7 in the right hand. 4×4=16, which added to 7 gives 23, of which place 3 in *the right hand in the place of hundreds*, and 2 in that hand *in the place of thousands.* Then the result is 2344.

Part 7. The same process with three figures. The example is 347×347.

Part 8. Introduced by a chapter on addition. This is the quadrilateral method (*in forma scacherii*). The example is to multiply 4321 by 567. The quadrilateral is divided into squares, so that the number of squares in each horizontal row is one more than the number of digits in the multiplicand, and the number in each vertical column is equal to the number of digits in the multiplier. Having multiplied the multiplicand by each digit of the multiplier, add the digits diagonally, beginning at the upper right hand corner.

2450007

4321

3	0	2	4	7	7
2	5	9	2	6	6
2	1	6	0	5	5

FIG. 8.

Proof: Check by nines.

XVII. ALEXANDER DE VILLA DEI.

Term. tech.: *multiplicare; multiplicandus; multiplicans; total numerus.*

Process: (1) Like II.

(2) To multiply digits by digits.

$$ab = 10a - a(10-b) \quad a<b$$

Proof: By division.

XVIII. SACROBOSCO.

Def. Multiplication is the process of finding from two numbers, a number which shall contain one of them as many times as there are units in the other.

Term. tech.: *multiplicare, multiplicatio; numerus multiplicans* (which is adverbial); *numerus multiplicandus* (which is nominal); *productus, summa.*

Either number may be used as the multiplier.

There are six rules of multiplication.

(1) To multiply digits by digits.

$$ab = 10a - a(10-b) \quad a<b.$$

Example: $4 \times 8 = 40 - 4 \times 2$.

(2) To multiply a digit by an article.

$b \times 10a = (ab)\ 10$, using Rule (1)

(3) To multiply a digit by a composite number.

$c(10a+b) = (ac)10 + bc$, using Rules (1) and (2).

(4) To multiply an article by an article.

Multiply the significant figures. If this product is in the units place the result is hundreds, if in tens place, the result is thousand.

(5) To multiply articles by composite numbers.

Multiply the article by each part of the composite number and add the results.

(6) To multiply any composite number by any other composite number.

(a) Multiply each part of the multiplier by each part of the multiplicand and add the results (Cf. VIII. (2)).

(b) The method of Al-Khowarizmi. The figures of the multiplicand are erased and replaced by those of the product.

Proof: Divide the product by one of the factors.

XIX. SALEM CODEX.

Term. tech.: *multiplicare, multiplicatio; multiplicandus; multiplicans; summa.*

Process: A knowledge of the products up to 5×5 is presupposed. (*Quis enim non scita, quod quinquas 5 sunt 25? Quater quatuor sunt 16 . . .*)

(1) To multiply digits by digits, when greater than 5.

$$ab=[b-(10-a)]\,10+(10-a)\,(10-b).$$

Example: $9\times9=(9-1)\,10+1\times1=81$.

Differentia is used as in XII, to indicate the difference between 10 and the given number. In the application of the rule a is not necessarily greater than b.

(2) To square a digit: $a^2=10\,(a-d)+d^2$ where $d=10-a$.

Example: $8\times8=10(6)+2^2$.

(3) A suggestion, but not a rule for the multiplication of any digit by 9; $9a=10a-a$.

Example: $9\times9=90-9$; $8\times9=80-8$.

(4) Like II. The result replaces the multiplicand.

Proof: Check by nines.

XX. AL-BANNA.

Def. Multiplication is the repetition of one of two numbers as many times as there are units in the other.

Process: (1) Multiplication by translation.

(a) By the horizontal: like II, the product replacing the upper number.

(b) By the vertical: the same process with the numbers written vertically so that the first digit of one factor is *beside* the last digit of the other. No examples are given.

(2) Multiplication by demi translation—to be used only when the numbers are identical. The process is that used in the squaring of a polynomial by means of the formula. $(a+b+c+\ldots)^2=a^2+2ab+b^2+2ac+2bc+c^2+\ldots$

No example is given. (Cf. XXXVII.)

(3) Multiplication without translation.

(a) Quadrilateral method. The quadrilateral is divided into squares, through which diagonals are drawn from the upper angle at the left to the lower angle at the right. The multiplicand is written above and the multiplier at the left. Multiply each figure of the multiplicand by each figure of the multiplier placing units above and tens below the diagonal. Add the numbers between the diagonals.[1]

(b) By vertical: draw two vertical lines, leaving a space between. Write the two numbers along the lines. Multiply successively the digits of one number by all the digits of the other, placing the results in the space between as their order demands.

(c) By horizontal: place the numbers in two parallel lines. Multiply each digit of one by every digit of the other, beginning either at the right or the left, and write the results as their order demands.[2]

[1] No example is given, but in a note the translator states that the multiplication of 265 by 28 would be performed as follows.

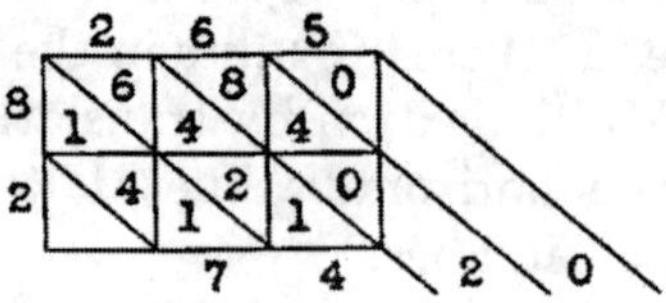

[2] Possibly like VIII (2).

(4) Multiplication by multiples: If the two factors have the same number of digits, and each is a succession of equal digits, write the numbers so that the first digit of one shall be under the last digit of the other. Write the numbers 1, 2, 3 . . . under these beginning at the right, until the last digit of the upper number. Then diminish by 1 and continue until the last of the lower number. Multiply the result by the product of the repeated numbers.[1]

(5) By excess: Take the excess of one number over ten, divide by 10, multiply by the other number, add that number and multiply by ten, i.e., $ab=\left[\frac{a-10}{10}.b+b\right]10.$[2]

(6) By denomination.

(a) Divide one of the two factors by their sum, multiply by the other, and by their sum, i.e., $ab=\left(\frac{a}{a+b}\times b\right)(a+b).$

(b) Like VIII. 3 (a) and (b).

(7) To multiply a sequence of nines by a sequence of any other digit, the two sequences having the same number of digits. Make as many dots as the sum of all the digits. Write the units of the product of the repeated digits on the first dot, and the tens on the middle one of the remaining dots. On the dots between these numbers write the difference between the repeated digits, and on the other dots the digit of the number which is not the sequence of nines.[3]

(8) (a) Like VIII. (5)

(b) Like VIII. (8)

[1] No example is given, but the translator states that the product of 777×666 would be found as follows.

$$\begin{array}{r} 777 \\ 666 \\ \hline 12321 \end{array} \quad : \quad 42(12321)=\text{the product.}$$

[2] Eneström suggests that the translation is incorrect at this point and sees here a possible trace of complementary multiplication. *Cf. Bibl. Math. VII₃ p. 96.*

[3] This would be illustrated as follows: To multiply 333 by 999, make 6 dots, beginning at the right, put 7 on the first dot and 2 on the fourth. Write 6 on the second and third, and 3 on the fifth and sixth, thus $\underset{\cdots\cdots}{332667}$.

(9) (a) Symbolized as follows $ab = a^2 - a(a-b) : a > b$.

(b) Symbolized as follows $ab = b^2 + b(a-b) : a > b$.

(10) When the figures on the right are zeros, cut them off and annex them to the product of the remaining numbers.

(11) The discussion of multiplication closes with the statements that the number of digits in a product cannot exceed the number in the multiplier added to the number in the multiplicand, and that the result of a multiplication may be proved by division. Finally the author gives a multiplication table in the following form.

2 by 2 is 4, and for each succeeding product add 2
3 by 3 is 9, and for each succeeding product add 3
etc. up to
10 by 10 is 100, and for each succeeding product add 10.

XXI. OCREATUS.

Term. tech.: *multiplicare; multiplicandus; multiplicans.*

Process: (1) To square a number less than 10, $a^2 = (a-d)\,10 + d^2$ when $d = 10 - a$[1].

Example: $9 \times 9 = 8 \times 10 + 1$. $a-d$ is called the *arithmetica medietas* between a and 10. Thus 9×9 will differ from 8×10 by the product of 1×1. Similarly 8×8 will be equal to $6 \times 10 + 2 \times 2$, and 7×7 will be equal to $4 \times 10 + 3 \times 3$.

(2) If a number is a geometrical mean between two others its square is equal to the product of those numbers. Example 20×20 is equal to 4×100. If one of the extremes is 100 the other is found by taking such a part of *a* as *a* is of 100, i.e., 60 is the geometrical mean between 36 and 100 because 60 is $^3/_5$ of 100, and $^3/_5$ of 60 is 36.

(3) To multiply any digit by 9.

(a) $9a = 10a - 1a$; ex. $7 \times 9 = 7 \times 10 - 7 \times 1$.

(b) $9a = a^2 + a(9-a)$; ex. $7 \times 9 = 7 \times 7 + 7 \times 2$.

(4) To multiply two numbers find the product of the *limit* of the order and a number which bears the same ratio to one

[1] The Rule of Nikomachus.

of the numbers that the other bears to the *limit*. Ex. $5\times 6=10 \times 3$ because $3:5=6:10$. Other examples are given.

(5) To multiply any number by another: The smaller number is written below the other, and multiplication begins at the left. Roman numbers are used in the process of multiplying 33 by 33, which is carried on as in II.

XXII. ALGORITHMUS DEMONSTRATUS.

Def. To multiply is to take one number as many times as there are units in the other.

Term. tech.: *multiplicare, multiplicatio; multiplicandus; multiplicans; numerus productus.*

The explanation of the process consists of a sequence of propositions (XIII–XX) each depending upon those preceding. Each contains a statement and a proof, after the Euclidean model, using letters. They may be represented as follows:

XIII. Complementary multiplications $ab=10a-a(10-b)$.

If two digits multiplied together give a digit, i.e., if $a\times b=c$.

XIV. $a\times 10^n b=10^n c$.

XV. $10^n a\times 10^m b=10^r c$; where $10^r : 10^m = 10^n : 1$

If two digits multiplied together give an article, i.e., if $a\times b=10c$.

XVI. $a\times 10^n b=10(10^n c)$.

XVII. $10^n.a\times 10^m b=10^r c$, where $10^r : 10^{n+1} = 10^n : 1$

If two digits multiplied together give a composite number, i.e., if $a\times b=10c+d$.

XVIII. $a\times 10^n b=10^{m+1}c+10^m d$.

XIX. $10^m(a)\times 10^n(b)=10^{r+1}(c)+10^r(d)$, where $10^r : 10^m = 10^n : 1$.

XX. To multiply any number by any other number. The method is that of II, propositions XIV–XIX being used to determine the order of the partial products. The process begins at the left and the figures of the multiplicand are erased in the process.

Ex. cba by ghk.[1]

Proof: Multiplication and division prove each other. (Prop. XXXI.)

XXIV. A THIRTEENTH CENTURY ALGORISM.

Def. To multiply is so to lead a number through another number by multiplying, that one result is obtained from the two.

Term. tech.: *multiplicato, multiplicare; multiplicandus; multiplicans; summa.*

Process: Like II. The greater number is usually placed above, though this is not necessary (*sola consuetudine et nulla necessitate*) and the product replaces the multiplicand.

Example: 432 by 12.

In the explanation of the process Roman numerals are used, only the statement and the final result appearing with the Hindu numerals.

Proof: By division, or check by nines.

XXV. PETRUS DE DACIA.

To illustrate Sacrobosco's definition.

5 by 4 is 20; 20 contains 5 as many times as 4 contains 1.
or 20 contains 4 as many times as 5 contains 1.

To illustrate the practical value of multiplication. "*Moreover this species is useful in such a case as follows: If a king should send to each soldier of an expedition, say 666, a sum of money, say 999 librae, to find the total sum.*

To illustrate XVIII. (1) Sacrobosco's example is repeated, and Dacia calls attention to the fact that the same rule holds for equal numbers.

Example: $8\times8=80-8\times2$.

[1] In the manuscript edited by Eneström, the latter factor is khg.

Dacia sees that Rules 2–5 are not necessary as an introduction to 6.b). He proceeds at once to the multiplication of 987 by 654, and of 45060 by 2030, according to the methods of II. and then returns to Rules 2–5 showing that they may be considered corollaries to 6, b).

Proof: In addition to the reverse operation as given by Sacrobosco, Dacia introduces the check by nines, the remainder after division being called *proba*. In case this is not considered conclusive, he suggests the check by eights, and says that if the result checks by both these methods, it is impossible that there should have been a mistake in the process.

XXVI. LEWI BEN GERSON.

The heading of the chapter on multiplication is *Of the addition of equal numbers, that is, of the multiplication of a number by another.*

Throughout the chapter the idea of the ratio is emphasized. The work begins with an extended discussion of the method of determining the order of a product, in which it is shown with many illustrations that the product of unity in the mth order by unity in the nth order is unity in the $m+n-1th$ order, because the ratio of the 1st order to the mth order is equal to the ratio of the nth order to the $m+n-1th$ order.

Process: (1) The method is that of the present time except that the upper number is used as a multiplier. Ben Gerson states that either factor may be chosen as multiplier but that it is more convenient to choose that containing the less number of digits. The example given is shown in Fig. 9.

```
      7000030
       180640
      -------
      5419200
1264480
-------------
1264485419200
```

FIG. 9.

(2) To find the square of a number, write it under itself and proceed as in (1). To find the cube multiply the square by the number.

(3) A method which if $a \pm x$ is an article, may be symbolized as follows:

$$ab = (a \pm x)(b \mp x) \pm \{(a \pm x) - b\}x;$$
$$ab = (b \pm x)(a \mp x) \mp \{(a - (b \pm x)\}x; \ a > b$$

Example: $57 \times 34 = 60 \times 31 + 26 \times 3.$
$57 \times 34 = 50 \times 41 - 16 \times 7.$
$57 \times 34 = 40 \times 51 - 17 \times 6.$
$57 \times 34 = 30 \times 61 + 27 \times 4.$

It is stated that this method is convenient when $(a \pm x) = (b \pm x)$.

Example: $43 \times 57 = 50 \times 50 + 7 \times 7.$

(4) $ab = (a \pm x)b \mp xb$

Example: $57 \times 34 = 60 \times 34 - 3 \times 34.$
$57 \times 34 = 50 \times 34 + 7 \times 34.$

(5) $a^2 = (a + x)\ (a - x) + x^2$

Example: $47 \times 47 = 50 \times 44 + 9.$

(6) To square a number: Find its ratio to the unit of the next order, multiply the number by this ratio and by the unit of the next order.

Example: $30^2 = 3/10 \times 30 \times 100.$ (Cf. VIII. 3a.)

(7) To square a number of two digits: $a^2 = (a \mp x)^2 \pm \{(a \mp x) + a\}x.$

Example: $33^2 = 30^2 + 63 \times 3.$
$32^2 = 40^2 - 73 \times 7.$

(8) Like XIV. (3).

The example given is 33^2. According to the rule, $33^2 = 10(11)^2 - 121 = 1210 - 121$. It is stated that this is true because the ratio of the square of 33 to the square of 11 is the same as the ratio of the side of one square to the side of the other square, multiplied by itself. But the ratio of the sides, multiplied by itself is 9 : 1, therefore the square of 33 is 9 times the square of 11. But 1210 is 10 times the square of 11, hence it is necessary to subtract the square of 11.

XXVIII. PLANUDES.

Def. Multiplication takes place when one number measures another as often as there are units in the measuring number, and from this measuring there results another number.

Process:

(1) Cross multiplication, treated much as it is given in the *Liber abaci*. There is, however, no suggestion of finger symbolism, the figure to be carried being held *in the mind* instead of *in the hand*. The smaller number is not always written above the greater. Multiplication of a digit by another directly above it he calls *simple multiplication*, and the double multiplication of the nth digit with the mth is called multiplication *over the cross*.

(a) 2 figures by 2 figures. Example:

840
24
35

(b) 3 figures by 3 figures. Example:

114048
432 264

(c) In case one factor contains a greater number of digits, than are in the other, write zero at the left of the smaller number until the number of digits is the same.

Example:

76842
1423 0054

(d) The general rule. The explanation is equivalent to the following.

When multiplying the 1st and nth digits there will be n partial products to add. If n is even, all of these will be *over the cross*, if n is odd there will be one *simple* multiplication. When all the multiplications beginning with the first digit have been completed, make a mark over it and proceed to the second, being careful to omit those multiplications which have already been performed.

(2) Like II. Planudes states that this method is very difficult with paper and pen, but easy on a sandboard upon which the figures may be erased.

Example: 654 by 654. The product takes the place of the upper number.

Proof: Check by nines.

XXIX. JOHN DE MURIS.

The *Quadripartitum* is a work upon abacus reckoning, but in the description of the process of multiplication is found the rule used by the algorists (and also by Abraham ben Esra) for determining the order of a product, namely, to subtract 1 from the sum of the orders of the factors. The example given is to multiply 365 (the number of days in a year), by 24 (the number of parts of a day), to find the number of hours in a year. The process begins at the left, and 365 is multiplied first by 2 and then by 4, the position of the products upon the abacus being determined by the rule given above.

XXXII. ALGORISMUS PROSAYCUS.

Def. Multiplication is increasing one number by another as many times as there are units in the other.

Term. tech.: *multiplicacio, multiplicare; numerus multiplicandus; numerus multiplicans; numerus productus.*

Process: Like II. Either number may be used as the multiplier.

Example: 6504 by 207. The result replaces the upper number.

Note: A square and a triangular multiplication table are inserted between the work on integers and the fragment on fractions.

XXXIII. BELDAMANDI.

Def. (1) Multiplication is leading a number into itself or into another number, so that a third number results.

(2) Multiplication is finding a third number which will contain one of two numbers as many times as the other contains unity.

Term. tech.: *multiplicare, multiplicatione; numerus multiplicandus; multiplicans; summa totius multiplicationis.*

Process: The author states that the *ancients* say that either number may be used as a multiplier, but that it is better to use the smaller.

(1) To multiply digits by digits; $ab = 10b - (10 - a)b$.

(2) A method exactly like that of the present day. The multiplier having been written below the multiplicand, multiply each digit of the multiplicand by the units digit of the multiplier, then using the tens digit of the multiplier proceed as before, remembering that each partial product must precede that next below it by one figure, and that multiplication by zero gives nothing. The example is given in Fig. 10.

```
    6204
    5073
   -----
   18612
  43428
 0000
31020
--------
31472892
```

FIG. 10.

Proof: Check by nines.

XXXIV. KILLINGWORTH.

. Term.. tech: *multiplicatio; numerus multiplicandus; numerus multiplicans; productus.*

Process: Essentially like II, though the arrangement of the work is complicated by grouping the digits of the multiplier as far as possible in pairs. A peculiarity is found in the use of the calculating slates (*lapis calculatoris*). Each number is written upon a slate and the greater (the multiplicand) is placed on the under slate above the smaller (the multiplier) in such a way that the digit of highest order is above the units digit of the multiplier. The digits of the multiplier are then multiplied in pairs as noted above, by the last digit of the multiplicand, and the partial products are written below on the lower slate, in a column corresponding to the digit of the multiplier. Next, the top slate is moved one place to the right and the process is repeated. The result is obtained by adding the partial products, although this is not stated explicitly in the manuscript. The illustrative problems give only multiplicand, multiplier, product and check by nines with no intermediate steps.

A multiplication table appears in which are given the products by 1–9 of numbers 1–99.[1]

XXXV. A FIFTEENTH CENTURY ALGORISM.

A multiplication table is given in the form of a square. After the different cases of multiplication of one and two place numbers, there follows the multiplication *in schachir*. At the end of the chapter are given two examples of the multiplication of nine place factors by the method *per gelosia*.[2]

XXXVI. A GERMAN ALGORISM.

Term. tech.: *multiplicio, multipliceren; numerus multiplicandus; numerus multiplicans; numerus die daer aff coemt.*

Process: (1) Complementary multiplication

(a) $ab = 10a - (10-b)a;\ a < b.$

Example: $8 \times 9 = 80 - 8(1)$

(b) $a^2 = 10a - (10-a)a.$

(2) To multiply tens, remove the zeros, multiply the remaining digits, and make a hundred from each unit of the product.

(3) Like II. In the process the product takes the place of the multiplicand (written above).

Proof: Divide the product by the multiplier.

[1] See p. 52, note.

[2] I assume that the methods *in schachir* and *per gelosia* are those found in Pacciuolo's *Summa*. There is nothing to show how the multiplications of one and two place factors are performed.

XXXVII. AL-KALCADI.

Def. Multiplication is the process of finding an unknown number from two known numbers.

Process: (1) Inclined multiplication. This is essentially the method of II. The example given, to multiply 52×73, is shown in Fig. 11. There is no mention of any erasure. A second example is 9736×582.

```
  3796
     6
    14
   15
 35
   |52
   73
    73
```

FIG. 11.

(2) Multiplication by means of place values. Multiply one of the factors by each digit of the other and place a dot over each figure as it is used for a multiplier. The example given, to multiply 321×432 is shown in Fig. 12. A second example is 1543×7852.

```
138672
1284
 963
 642
 432
 321
```

FIG. 12.

(3) Multiplication by demi transposition. Like XX, 2. Al-Kalçadi squares 438 and 556, the explanations being rhetorical, and following the formula $(a+b+c\ldots)^2 = a^2+2ab+b^2+2ac+2bc+c^2\ldots$ In a note Woepcke illustrates the process as in Fig. 13. To square 438, first the square of 4 is written above the 4, then 2×4 is written below the dot which separates the digits of the number to be squared, and the product of this by 3 is written above the dot. Next the square of 3 is written above the 3. the 8 is moved one place to the right, and 2×3 is written below the next dot. Then 8 and 6 are multiplied by 8, the results being written above the corresponding numbers, and finally the square of 8 is written above the 8. The final result is 191844.

```
191844
    64
   48
   64
   9
  24
 16
 4.3.8
  886
```

FIG. 13.

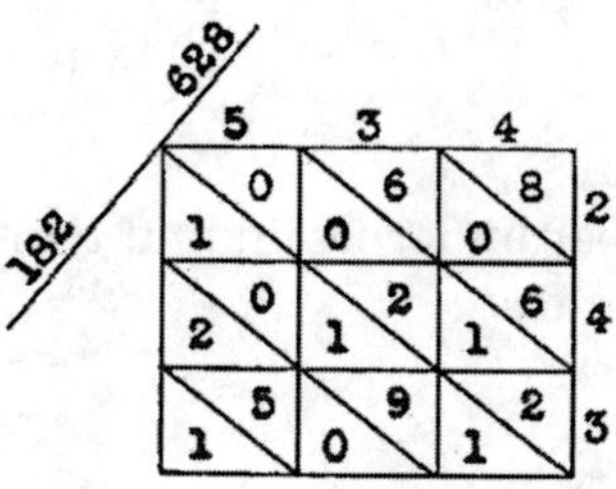

FIG. 14.

(4) The method of *reseau*. A quadrilateral method as shown in Fig. 14. The multiplicand is placed above, the

multiplier at the right, and the product at the upper left hand corner. Fig. 14 shows the multiplication of 342×534. Another example is the multiplication of 64×3 performed in the same way.

(5) Following the statement that a knowledge of the products of digits is necessary there is a paragraph giving in words the methods of finding the products from 2×2 up to 13×13, as in XX. (11).

(6) The concluding paragraph gives rules which may be useful in certain cases.

Any number multiplied by zero is zero.

Any number multiplied by unity is itself.

To multiply a number by 2, add it to itself.

To multiply a number by 3, add it to its double.

To multiply a number by 4, double the double.

To multiply a number by 5, annex 0 and take a half.

To multiply a number by 6, add it to half the product by 10.

The rules given for the multiplication by 7, 8, 9 might be reduced to the formula for complementary multiplication. $ab = 10a - (10 - b)a$; $b = 7, 8, 9$.

To multiply a number by 99, add two zeros and subtract the number.

To multiply by 10, annex one zero; to multiply by 100, annex two zeros.

To multiply by 11, add the number to itself after changing the order.

Ex. 352 × 11, add 352
352

To multiply by 12, place the number under itself, and then write it a third time changing the order.

Ex. 34×12, add 34
34
34
408

To multiply by 15, add the number to its half if it is an even number, and annex one zero; if it is odd, subtract one, add half of the remainder to the original number, and annex 5.

Ex. 24×15; $24+12=36$. Result 360:
9×15; $9+4=13$. Result 135.

To multiply any number by a sequence of two equal digits, multiply by one of the equal digits and add the result to itself, changing the order. Ex. 31×22, add 62

$$\begin{array}{r} 62 \\ \underline{62} \\ 682 \end{array}$$

XXXVIII. PEURBACH.

Def. Multiplication is the process of finding a number which shall contain one of two numbers as many times as the other contains unity.

Term. tech.: *multiplicare, multiplicatio; numerus superior; numerus inferior; productus.*

Process: (1) The necessity of being able to multiply digits is emphasized, and a table of products up to 9×9 is given. There appears also the rule for complementary multiplication $ab = 10a - (10-b)a$; $a < b$.

(2) To multiply numbers with several digits, it is advisable to place the smaller number below. The process is that used at the present time.

Proof: Check by nines.

SECTION IX.

Division.

The subject of division as treated in most of the works of this period shows little variety or originality. In the definition, which emphasizes the idea of ratio, the Greek influence is apparent; but the process of operation is that used by the Hindus. The removal of common factors from dividend and divisor, the separation of the dividend into parts and the repeated division by factors of the divisor are found in some of the Arabic treatises. The *Liber abaci* also considers some of these, but they do not appear in any of the other Latin algorisms examined. The arithmetic of Al-Karkhi makes no attempt to explain the arrangement of the example, but his idea is modern, and the fact that Lewi ben Gerson failed to see the greater convenience of writing remainders below, rather than above the dividend is all that prevents his method from being that used at the present time.

With these exceptions however, all the works examined treat the subject of division in the same way. The earlier algorisms, influenced by sand table and abacus reckoning, actually replace the dividend by the remainder; but later by drawing lines through the figures used, and writing the remainders above, the *scratch* or *galley* method was developed. Minor variations occur in the position of the quotient and the divisor, but in general the method that Al-Khowarismi received from the Hindus is the same as that commonly used at the end of the 15th century.

II. ALGORITMI DE NUMERO INDORUM.

Term. tech.: *divisio, dividere; superior numerus quem dividis; inferior numerus super quem dividis.*

Process: (1) To divide a number of several digits by another number of several digits: Write the divisor under the dividend so that the digit of highest order shall be under that of highest order in the dividend. In case the left hand digit of the divisor is greater than that of the dividend, move the divisor one place to the right.

Find a number which when multiplied by the digit of highest order in the divisor, will give a product equal to or less than the number above it, and write this number above (or below if more convenient) the units digit of the divisor. Multiply each digit of the divisor by the quotient, beginning at the left, and having subtracted the products replace the digits of the dividend by the remainders.[1] When every digit of the divisor has been multiplied by the quotient, move the divisor one place to the right and proceed as before. The process is continued until the units digit of the divisor stands under the units digit of the dividend.

```
  143
    1
   12
  113
  224
14006
46468
324
 324
  324
```

FIG. 1.

Example: To divide 46468 by 324. The explanation given in the text is wholly rhetorical, but following the instructions, the example would stand as shown in Fig. 1. The quotient is 143 and the remainder is 136. The figures of the dividend having been erased and replaced by those above them, the completed example would stand as in Fig. 2. showing only quotient and remainder.

```
  143
  136
324
 324
  324
```

FIG. 2.

(2) The division of a number of several digits by a number of one digit: The division of 1800 by 9 is performed first exactly as in (1), but the statement is made later that if there are zeros at the right of a number, they may be removed and annexed to the quotient.

Proof: No proof appears, but the author recognizes that there is a relation between multiplication and division for he says *Et scito quod diuisio sit similis multiplicatione* p. 14.

[1] That the dividend is erased and replaced by the remainder, I infer from the statement *ponemusque in loco eius* which occurs in the illustrative example. p. 15.

III. MAHAVIRACARYA.

Process: (1) "Put down the dividend, and divide it, in accordance with the process of removing common factors, by the divisor which is placed below that (dividend), and then give out the resulting (quotient)."

(2) "The dividend should be divided in the reverse way (i.e. from left to right) after performing in relation to (both of) them the operation of removing common factors, if that be possible."

Example: Nine examples are stated, without solutions. The first is as follows: *8192 dinaras have been divided among 64 men. What is the share of one man?*

V. SRIDHARACARYA.

Like III (2). No example, or proof.

VI. AL-NASAWI.

The analysis states that Chapters 10 and 11 contain the definition, the kinds of division, a description of the process, and the proof. In a note Woepcke gives the division of 2852 by 12 as performed by Al-Nasawi, as shown in Fig. 3. Here 237 is the quotient, and 8 the remainder. This process is similar to II (1).

```
  12
 498
 237
2852
12
 12
  12
```

Fig. 3.

VII. AVICENNA.

No example is given, but the statement is made that the check by nines may be used to verify the result.

VIII. AL-KARKHI.

Def. (1) Division is the process of finding how many times the divisor may be added to itself in order to produce the dividend.

(2) Division is seeking for the parts of the whole.

(3) Division is the process of finding the number which when multiplied by the divisor, will produce the dividend.

In this case unity must be to the quotient as the divisor is to the dividend.

Process: The process is explained by means of an example. To divide 20325 by 125, find among the hundreds the greatest number that multiplied by 135 will give the dividend·or something less. That is 100, and the product is 13500. Subtract 13500 from 20325 and the remainder is 6825. Now find among the tens, the greatest number which multiplied by 135 will give 6825 or less. This is 50, and the product is 6750. Subtract 6750 from 6825, and the remainder is 75. If this had been greater than 135, it would have been necessary to find a unit. But since that is not the case, find a fraction which multiplied by 135 gives 75. This is 75/135 or 5/9 and therefore the result is 150 5/9.

IX. AL-HASSAR.

Al-Hassar is one of the writers who considers two kinds of division, i.e., that of a smaller by a greater number, which is simply finding the ratio of one number to a greater, and that of a greater by a smaller number.

In the work on division of a larger by a smaller number, 98746 is divided by 36, by dividing by 4×9, the result being written 2742 $\frac{8}{9}\frac{2}{4}$ ($2742+\frac{8}{9}+\frac{2}{36}$).[1] The check by sevens is used.

X. BHASKARA.

Process: "That number, by which the divisor being multiplied balances the last digit of the dividend (and so on), is the quotient in division; or if practicable, first abridge both the divisor and dividend by an equal number, and proceed to division."[2]

Example: Here the product found in the example to illustrate multiplication is used for a dividend, and the multi-

[1] A similar method of writing fractions is found in the works of Abu Kamil, and other Arabic writers, and also in those of Leonard of Pisa.

[2] A note states that *and so on* implies repeating the divisor for every digit of the quotient.

plier for a divisor. Dividing 1620 by 12 the quotient is 135, the same as the original multiplicand; or dividing both numbers by **3** the problem is to divide 540 by 4; or dividing both by 4, the problem is to divide **405** by 3. The quotient in all cases is 135.

XI. LIBER ALGORISMI.

Def. To divide a number by a number is to distribute the greater in accordance with the size of the smaller. that is, to take away the smaller from the greater as many times as possible.

Term. tech.: *dividere; dividens; dividendus.*

Process: This work imposes the condition that the dividend must be greater than the divisor. The process is like II (1).

968
156
236

Fig. 4.

Example: 228604.
236

The result is written after the Hindu fashion as in Fig. 4. by which is meant 968 156/236.

The second example, 1800 appears also in II.
9

Proof: Check by nines, or by multiplication.

XII. A TWELFTH CENTURY ALGORISM.

Term. tech.: *divisio, dividere; dividendus; dividens, divisor.*

Process: Like II (1). The figures of the dividend are erased in the course of the division.

Example: 25920
24

The final result stands
1080
000, in
24

which 1080 is the quotient and 0 is the remainder.

Proof: By multiplication.

XIV. ABRAHAM BEN ESRA.

Process: The statement is made that unless dealing with fractions, the dividend must be greater than the divisor.

Write the divisor under the dividend, units under units, etc., and leave a line between in which to write the quotient. Except for these modifications the method is the same as in II (1).

Example:

```
  0
019
120
2154
8213
  23
353
```

This illustrates the division of 8213 by 353. The quotient is 23 and the remainder 94.

Several other examples are given, but no new principle is introduced. The last is the division of 777777777 by 9999.

Proof: Check by nines.

XV. DEMONSTRATIO JORDANI DE ALGORISMO.

Def. To divide is to find a number which shall be contained in the dividend as many times as the divisor contains unity.

Term. tech.: *dividere; dividendus, numerus superior; divisor, numerus inferior.*

Process: Like II (1). No example is given.

Proof: By multiplication.

XVI. LEONARD OF PISA.

Term. tech.: *dividere, divisio.*

Process: (1) Introduced by a division table in which the divisors are the numbers 1–13 (except 10), and the quotients are 10 or less. This table is followed by examples using these numbers as divisors, the process being that of short division as taught today. Fractions are written at the left. The division of 365 by 2 is as follows.

```
  365
    2
 ½182.
```

(2) The same process carried on mentally with the help of finger symbolism.

(3) To divide by 10, erase the units digit and write it above 10, at the left of the number. Thus 167 divided by 10 is $\frac{7}{10}$ 16.

	1432
	2913122
	780005
	59
$\frac{25}{59}$	13220

Fig. 5.

(4) To divide by prime numbers of two digits the process is like that of II (1) except that the units digit of the divisor is written under the units digit of the dividend. Several examples are given, among them that shown in Fig. 5, which illustrates the division of 78005 by 59. The quotient is 13220 $\frac{25}{59}$.

(5) To divide by a composite number; separate it into its prime factors and divide by these in turn. A table containing the composite numbers less than 100 is followed by illustrative examples.

(6) The division by prime numbers of three and four figures: as in (4).

Proof: Check by nines or elevens, or by multiplication.

XVII. ALEXANDER DE VILLA DEI.

Term. tech.: *dividere; major numerus; minor numerus.*

Process: Like II (1). No examples or proof.

XVIII. SACROBOSCO.

Def. Division is the process of distributing one number in as many parts as there are units in another.

Term. tech.: *dividere, divisio; numerus dividendus; numerus dividens, divisor; numerus denotans quotiens, numerus exiens.*

Process: Like II (1). No example.

Proof: By multiplication.

XIX. SALEM CODEX.

Def. Division is the determination of the number of times a smaller number is repeated in a greater.

Term. tech.: *divisio; dividendus; dividens.*

Process: Like II (1).

Example: 1432. No proof is given.
19

XX. AL-BANNA.

Def. Division is the decomposition of a dividend into equal parts, the number of parts being equal to the number of units in the division.

Process: Two cases are considered.

(1) When the dividend is less than the divisor. Reduce the denominator to its prime factors and divide the numerator by one or more of these, if possible.

(2) When the dividend is greater than the divisor.

(a) Place the divisor under the dividend, then find a number (and place it below the units digit of the divisor), which when multiplied by the divisor will destroy the dividend, or leave a remainder less than the divisor. This remainder is to be reduced by (1).

(b) Separate the dividend into its parts, divide each of them by the divisor and add the results.

(c) Divide the dividend by the factors of the divisor.

(d) Separate both dividend and divisor with factors, divide and multiply.[1]

XXI. OCREATUS.

Term. tech.: *divisere, divisio.*

Process: Roman numerals are used exclusively, both in the text and in the illustrative examples, the zero being represented by τ or $\bar{o}$. The examples show the division of 1089 by 33, and of 140000 by 1200, both used to prove the results of the work on multiplication, and of 148 by 16. The process seems to be that of II (1).

XXIV. A THIRTEENTH CENTURY ALGORISM.

Def. To divide is to distribute many among few, in order to find what part of the dividend is equal to the divisor.

Term. tech.: *dividere; dividendus, major numerus; divisor, minor numerus.*

Process: Like II (1).

[1] Ordinary cancellation.

Example: To divide "octingente XXX.IIII^or marce inter XXXIIII^or milites."

The problem is written

8.3.4
3 4

in which the remainder 18 replaces the dividend, and the quotient 24 is written above.

and the result

24
18
34

Proof: By multiplication, or check by nines.

XXV. PETRUS DE DACIA.

The text of Sacrobosco is illustrated by two examples, the first of which is the division of 9876 by 543. The final result is given in the form

18,
102
543

in which 18 is the quotient, and the remainder 102 has replaced the dividend. The second example 78876 divided by 38 is inserted to illustrate the case in which there is a zero in the quotient.

6212
72271
544121
6206321
43954321
987654321
104657
9437
943700000
37448000
5662200
471850
66059

Fig. 6.

Dacia uses the check by nines, as well as that by multiplication which is the method used in the *Algorismus vulgaris*.

XXVI. LEWI BEN GERSON.

The chapter on division begins as follows: "You know that every product contains one of the factors as many times as there are units in the other. Therefore, if you know the product and one factor, it is possible to find the other factor."

Process: Here as in his treatment of the other operations the writer is most advanced, the process except in arrangement being that used at present. The dividend is 987654321, the divisor is 9437, the quotient is 104657 and the remainder is 6212. In finding the first digit of the quotient we are told to consider the dividend 9 and 8 tenths, and the divisor 9 and 5 tenths. The quotient, which is 1, must be written under the dividend in the place which is the fourth from the left, since 9 stands in the fourth place. The product is written below, and since 1 is in the 6th place, the units of the product will be in the 6th place also. Subtract the product 943700000 from the dividend, and write the remainder 43954321 above the dividend. Now 9 5 10 is not contained in 4 3 10, therefore write 0 in the quotient, and divide 43 9 10 by 9 5 10. The quotient, 4, is placed at the right of the other digits of the quotient. Multiply 9437 by 4, write the result below and subtract as before. The final result is 104657 with a remainder of 6212.

The author proceeds to explain that in case the digits of the divisor are identical with the same number of digits at the left of the dividend, it is unnecessary to consider the tenths. As an example he gives 9437 divided by 943.

XXVIII. PLANUDES.

Def. Division is the process of finding how many times one number contains another.

Process: There are three kinds of division.

(1) To divide a number by a greater number: Separate each unit of the smaller number into as many parts as there are units in the greater. For example, to divide 3 by 5, divide each unit of three into 5 parts, then in 3 there will be 15 of these parts i.e., fifteen fifths. Divide 15 by 5 and the result is three fifths. Sometimes it is possible to remove a common factor.

(2) A number divided by an equal number.

(3) A number divided by a greater number.

(a) When the divisor has one figure. Begin at the left and divide each digit of the dividend by the divisor.

1
4865
1621^{2}
3

Fig. 7.

Example: To divide 4865 by 3. The result is as in Fig. 7 in which 1621 is the quotient and 2 the remainder.

(b) When the divisor is an article and has two figures, or when the divisor has one figure and the dividend has a zero at the right.

(c) When the divisor is a composite number. Practically the same method as II (1). The quotient is written between dividend and divisor, and the remainder below. The example 856978 divided by 24 is written as in Fig. 8. Here the numbers 13, 16, 1, 17, are the remainders after subtracting 3 × 24 from 85, 5×24 from 136, 7×24 from 169, and 0×24 from 17. The numbers 2, 3, 2, 1, 3, are the remainders after subtracting 3×2 from 8, 5×2 from 13, 7×2 from 16, 0×2 from 1 and 7×2 from 17. The quotient is 35707 and the remainder is 10.

	13	16	1	17	
8^2	5^3	6^2	9^1	7^3	8
3	5	7	0	7	
2	4				10

Fig. 8.

XXXII. ALGORITHMUS PROSAYCUS.

Def. Division is distributing one number by means of a smaller or equal number.

Term. tech.: *divisio, dividere; numerus dividens; numerus dividendus; numerus quotiens.*

Process: Like II (1).

Ex. 91471800 divided by 2030 gives 46060.

Proof: Multiply quotient by divisor.

XXXIII. BELDAMANDI.

Def. Division is the process of finding how many times one number is contained in another, or

Division is the process of distributing one of two numbers into as many equal parts as there are units in the other.

Term. tech.: *dividere, divisio; numerus dividendus; numerus dividens; numerus quotiens.*

Process: Like II (1).

Example: To divide 97531 by 2468.

The solution is given as in Fig. 9, in which the quotient is 39 and the remainder 1279. Note that here in moving the divisor to the right, the last digit is written in the line above.

```
    2
   13
   587
  2345
  35709
 905531  (39
 24088
   240
```

Fig. 9.

XXXIV. KILLINGWORTH.

Term. tech.: *diuisio; numerus diuidendus; diuisor; quociens; remanens.*

The analysis states only that the process of division is carried on with variations of the ordinary method, analogous to those found in multiplication.

XXXV. A FIFTEENTH CENTURY ALGORISM.

The analysis states that the *upwards*, or *galley* method is used, and that some examples are given.

XXXVI. A GERMAN ALGORISM.

Term. tech.: *divisio, divideren; numerus dividendus, mesten numerus; numerus divisor, minsten numerus; numerus quociens.*

Process: Like II (1). No examples.

Proof: By multiplication.

XXXVII. AL-KALCADI.

Def. Division is the decomposition of a dividend into as many parts as there are units in the divisor. Each part will be to unity as the dividend is to the divisor.

Process: (1) To divide by a number of one digit. Like II (2).

Examples: 856 by 4 and 924 by 6. If there is a remainder, as in the division of 579 by 8, write the result $\frac{3}{8}$ 72.

(2) If the divisor is the product of factors, decompose it into its factors.

Example: 7365 divided by 15. Divide first by 3 and then by 5.

(3) To divide by 10. Place the last figure over ten, or if the last figure is 0, cut it off.

Example: 743 divided by 10 is $\frac{3}{10}$ 74

5360 divided by 10 is 532.

Note: Al-Kalçadi gives a chapter concerning the division of a smaller number by a greater, called in the translation *denomination*.

XXXVIII. PEURBACH.

Term. tech.: *dividere, divisio; dividendus; divisor; numerus quotiens.*

Process: Like II (1) The quotient is written at the right of the dividend, separated from it by a vertical line.

Proof: Check by nines, or by multiplication.

SECTION X.

Summary.

The origin of the methods of calculation known in India in the time of Aryabhatta have long been a matter of speculation. Through trade relations with China and Greece the scholars of India must have become familiar with the customs of those countries, and it would be strange if there were not some points of resemblance in the processes of computation. The Chinese arithmetic of Sun-Tsŭ, presumably much older than any existing Hindu work on mathematics, directs that in the process of multiplication the factors shall be so arranged that the units digit of one shall be below the digit of highest order of the other, that multiplication shall begin at the left, and that the multiplier shall be moved one place to the right after each partial product is found; and the same work states that when dividing, the divisor shall be drawn back one place after finding each digit of the quotient.[1] These methods are evidently similar to those of the Hindus, but if we remember that even when the Aryabhattiyam was written, the origin of Hindu calculation was so far in the past as to have been considered a divine gift, it is impossible to conclude that China contributed to the mathematical knowledge of India. Moreover, although multiplication as performed by Archimedes in his *Measurement of a circle*[2] is found in some of the Hindu treatises, these differ so essentially from the theoretical arithmetics of Nikomachus and Diophantos that the suggestion of Greek influence need hardly be considered.

Among the Hindus, mathematics was developed not as a subject of value in itself but as an aid to religious ceremonies or business transactions, consequently we find neither definition nor demonstration, but a mere setting forth in the most

[1] Y. Mikami, *The development of mathematics in China and Japan*, p. 28.
[2] Cf. T. L. Heath, *The works of Archimedes, Introduction*, p. lxxii.

cursory manner of the rules of calculation, which are performed mentally or on a board strewn with sand, the results only being retained.[1] All the works examined, though representing schools geographically widely separated, display this characteristic, and the Bakhshali manuscript, probably contemporary with the *Lilavati* shows a similar method of exposition.[2]

During the 7th century, upon the founding of the dynasty of the Caliphs in Bagdad, the learning of all the civilized world began to be absorbed by the Arabs. Translators were busied not only with such treatises as the great works of Euclid, Archimedes and Ptolemy, but also with the astronomy of Brahmagupta and the art of calculation known in India. Among the scholars attached to the court of Al-Mamun, early in the 9th century, was Mohammed ibn Musa Al-Khowarizmi who wrote an arithmetic and an algebra, and calculated tables for the use of astronomers. The arithmetic he distinctly ascribes to the Hindus, as does Al-Nasawi in his *Satisfactory treatise* written two centuries later, and as is done in the case of many other Arabic treatises.[3] Though retaining the essentials of the Hindu works, that of Al-Khowarizmi differs from them, both in arrangement and exposition. Beginning with the subject of numeration, the decimal system with the zero is explained at great length and the operations upon integers are discussed carefully and systematically.

Introductory treatises at hand, we find among the Arabs of the next few centuries a rapid development, as appears in the works of Al-Karkhi, Al-Banna, and Al-Kalcadi. It is evident that these writers were conversant with the learned works of the Greeks as well as with those of the Hindus, and upon the foundation derived from these sources they built a science full of ingenious methods and devices, showing them-

[1] G. R. Kaye, *Hindu mathematical methods*, *Bibl. Math.* XII₃ pp. 289–299.

[2] G. R. Kaye, *The Bakhshali Manuscript*, *Journal and proceedings of the Asiatic Society of Bengal*, (new series), VIII, pp. 349–361. Also A. F. R. Hoernle, *The Bakhshali Manuscript*, *Indian Antiquary*, XVIII, pp. 33-48.

[3] Smith-Karpinski. *The Hindu Arabic numerals*, p. 6.

selves to be true originators and not mere copyists transmitting to the middle ages the knowledge of the ancients.

The Hebrew works examined display characteristics similar to those of the Arabs, but the frequent references to Euclid and Nikomachus show that their authors were familiar with the writings of the Greek scholars. The *Sefer Massei Choscheb* of Lewi ben Gerson is exceedingly modern in its treatment of the fundamental operations; and the discussion of series and of permutations and combinations shows a degree of learning far in advance of his time.[1]

The arithmetic of Al-Khowarizmi found its way to the Arabs in Spain, where it was discovered by one of the translators of the 12th century. Upon his translation, or the Arabic manuscripts of the same work, and upon the arithmetic of Al-Karkhi, other arithmetics were based; and the type taking its name *algorism* from that of the Arab writer, was spread throughout the western world, where up to that time the abacus of Gerbert had been the ordinary means of calculation. Gradually the algorism displaced the abacus, but in the process absorbed something of the methods superseded, so that often, in expression or even in manner of operating we are reminded of mechanical calculation. Such words as *erigere*, *ponere* and *mutare* appear quite as if material counters were being used, and in the older treatises, the sum, remainder or product actually replaces one of the original numbers operated upon.

Yet the character of the arithmetic of the middle ages was not formed altogether by the work of Al-Khowarizmi, for at the critical time Leonard of Pisa, journeying through the east, found the more developed Arabic arithmetic, and returned to Europe to give to his countrymen, in the *Liber abaci*, methods which to him seemed better than those of the algorithm upon the column abacus.[2] Though this treatise,

[1] Tropfke does not mention Levi ben Gerson in his chapter on combinations.

[2] *Sed hoc totum etiam et algorismum atque arcus pictagore quasi errorem computaui respectu modi indorum*, *Liber Abaci*, p. 1.

from a mathematical point of view, was far superior to the translations of the work of Al-Khowarizmi, it seems not to have exerted so great an influence. This may have been because the western world was not yet ready for so advanced a treatise, or because the monks, copying from monastery to monastery spread the other type of algorism. Whatever the reason, it is a fact that of all the works examined only that of Planudes, shows marked resemblance to the *Liber abaci*, and it was not until the 16th century that its methods were commonly incorporated in the treatises on arithmetic. At the present time the importance of the work is fully recognized, and full descriptions of its contents have been published.[1]

This is not true, however, of the other algorisms, for investigation will show that very few of these receive more than a cursory description, and that no mention whatever is made of many whose importance is great. It is my purpose therefore, in closing this paper, to discuss briefly some of those algorisms which seemed to me influential in the development of methods of calculation, and to compare their relative importance.

The *Algoritmi de numero Indorum*, as has been established beyond doubt is a translation of the Arabic treatise of Al-Khowarizmi. The long explanation of numeration, wholly with the Roman letters, as well as the errors made in writing numbers according to the new system, show an unfamiliarity with the subject, and are evidences that the translation was one of the earliest, if not the first to appear in the Latin language. The word *caracter* which occurs often to designate the numerals was used by the followers of Gerbert, and *erigere* and *levare* suggest counters rather than the sand-table of the Arabs. It is indeed quite evident that the translator was using a language foreign to the subject he was introducing, in which the terms employed were applicable to the familiar abacus rather than to the Hindu methods.[2]

[1] Cantor, vol. II, pp. 1–35, gives an analysis of the work.
[2] This work is described by Cantor, vol. I, pp. 712–718.

The first part of the treatise known as the *Liber algorismi de pratica arismetrice* is similar to the translation mentioned above. That it dates from the 12th century is shown by the fact that the fragment on multiplication and division written by Ocreatus and dedicated to Adelard of Bath has its description of numeration copied from the former.[1] The *Liber algorismi* is much more complete in its demonstration and much more ready in the writing of numbers than is the *Algoritmi de numero Indorum,* and differs from the latter in several minor ways, such as the order of the operations of mediation and duplation, and the digits chosen to show the variation in the forms of the numerals. These in the older treatise are 5, 6, 7, 8, and in the *Liber algorismi* are 7 and 4. Nevertheless the works are strikingly similar in their treatment of the subject and probably both are based upon the same original. Though the later work is not a copy, it is clear from such passages as the following that the author of the *Liber algorismi* was familiar with the earlier translation.

. . . si nichil remanserit, pones circulum, ut non sit differentia uacua: set sit in ea circulus qui occupet ea, ne forte cum uacua fuerit, minuantur differentie, et putetur secunda esse prima. *Algoritmi de numero Indorum, p. 8.*	*Si nichil infra articulum remanserit, circulum scribes, qui differentiam occupet, ne forte cum uacua fuerit, differentie minuantur, et putetur prima que est secunda.* *Liber algorismi de pratica arismetrice, p. 30.*

The *Liber algorismi* includes a discussion of the extraction of roots, which is not found in the *Algoritmi de numero Indorum,* and until the end of this discussion (p. 93), proceeds logically from one subject to the next. Beginning at this point with the summation of series it is evidently made up of excerpts from other treatises in which there is little order and frequent repetition. As was shown in Section VIII, many of the methods of multiplication are found in the *Kâfî fîl Hisab* of Al-Karkhi, and it seems possible that other parts of the work may have been derived from the same source.

[1] Cf. Section IV of this paper.

Though in the first part of the treatise the zero is called *circulus*, we find later *ciffre* and *ziffre*,[1] which may indicate a different translator or a different word in the Arabic work translated. Whether John of Spain, Gerard of Cremona, or both collaborating, were the translators is still an open question, but the fact that Dominic Gundissallinus, who collaborated with John of Spain on several works refers to the *Liber algorismi* in his *De divisione philosophiae*[2] shows that the work must certainly have been known to John of Spain.

The 12th century algorism edited by Curtze consists of the first three books of an astronomical treatise, and could hardly be a translation of the Arabic treatise or treatises which were the bases of the algorisms described above. It was written evidently, only as an auxiliary to the study of astronomy, and did not exert any great influence upon later works. In his discussion of the possible authorship, Paul Tannery thinks it is such a treatise as might have been written by Adelard of Bath after a study of the arithmetic of Al-Khowarizmi.[3] Though the order of the operations is changed, no new methods are introduced if we except the table in triangular form which appears at the beginning of the chapter on multiplication.

The *Carmen de algorismo* written by Alexander de Villa Dei, was one of the most influential treatises of the period, as is shown not only by the great number of translations and copies extant, but by the similarity of treatment found in many later works. It is written in hexameter and in some places, especially in the discussion of the extraction of roots, the meaning of the text is difficult to determine. Nevertheless, possibly because it was written by the eminent grammarian whose *Doctrinale puerorum* had already become famous, the book was widely used. Translations into English, French

[1] pp. 113, 114.

[2] *Ex materia uero accidit ei aggregari et disgregari, multiplicari et diuidi et huiusmodi que docentur in libro algorismi*, *Beitrage z. Gesch. d. Philos. d. Millealters*, IV, no. 2-3, p. 91, Cf. L. C. Karpinski. *Augrim-stones*, *Modern Language Notes*, *Nov. 1912*.

[3] *Bibl. Math.* V_3, p. 116.

and Icelandic are known, and commentaries in English and Latin, as well as many Latin copies are to be found in the libraries of Europe. The arithmetical operations and the methods of performing them are those given in the *Liber algorismi* with which the author was evidently familiar. This is the first Latin work in which the number of operations is given definitely, and the first in which 0 is considered one of the numerals, for whereas the earlier treatises state that there are nine figures and a zero, *which signifies nothing*, the *Carmen de algorismo* states distinctly that the figures of the Hindus are *twice five*.

The *Algorismus vulgaris* of John of Sacrobosco is the work of a scholar and a teacher, and well deserves the great popularity it attained. Each subject is considered under its own heading, and the discussion of each operation is carried out logically beginning with a definition and proceeding to an exposition of the process. In his description of the work Cantor refers to it as a collection of rules without demonstration, example or indication of the sources from which they were derived, and gives the impression that it was of little importance compared with the *Algorithmus demonstratus*.[1] The two differ essentially, however, in their purpose, and necessarily in their content and it is difficult to compare them. The *Algorismus vulgaris* was not written as a theoretical text for philosophers, but as a practical exposition of the art of reckoning, to be used in the universities of the period. When combined as was customary, with oral teaching or with a commentary such as that of Petrus de Dacia, who explains and illustrates the text most clearly, it was eminently fitted for this object, and that its value was appreciated is shown by the great number of manuscripts that are to be found in most collections of mathematical works, and by the extensive use of it which was made by later writers.

A scholar in the position of John of Sacrobosco could not fail to have been acquainted with the earlier Latin algorisms,

[1] Cantor: vol. II ed. 1900, p. 88.

and the quotation appearing in his chapter on duplation is proof that the *Carmen de algorismo* must have been at hand. The emphasis laid upon the possibility of beginning to add or subtract either at the right or left is found also in the *Liber algorismi de pratica arismetrice*, and though the two works differ in the words used, the ideas are so similar that I insert the following quotations:

> *Potes tamen et in agregatione ab ultima differentia incipere, et in diminutione a prima, uel in utraque ab ultima, uel in utraque a prima, si uolueris. Attamen si facilius fiet, ut in exemplis supra monstratum est.*
>
> *Liber algorismi*, p. 35.

> *Sciendum tamen, quod tam in additione quam in subtractione possumus bene a sinistra incipere redeundo versus dextram; sed tamen, ut prius dicebatur, est commodosius; ut praedictum est.*
>
> *Algorismus vulgaris*, p. 5.

If Sacrobosco knew Arabic treatises other than that of Al-Khowarizmi, as is quite possible, the reason for his introduction of *Progressions* as one of the *Species* is evident, for series play an important part in many of these Arabic works. The subject is found indeed in the latter half of the *Liber algorismi*. Though the *Liber algorismi* emphasizes the Hindu origin of the numerals, it states that among those following the Arabs (*aput Arabes sequentem, p. 35*) the tens digit of the article is transferred to the order on the left, a statement which may have been responsible for Sacrobosco's assertion that the Arabs were the inventors of the science of calculation. He does not state that the numerals originated among the Arabs, but through the wide-spread use of the *Algorismus vulgaris*, the idea of the Arabic origin of the processes became common, and it is probably due to its influence that at the present day the numerals are known as the Arabic rather than Hindu.[1]

The Salem Codex, the date of which Cantor places at 1200 or earlier, contains nothing which is not found also in the *Carmen de algorismo* or the *Algorismus vulgaris*, except its philosophical and ecclesiastical applications. It limits the

[1] Cf. Smith-Karpinski, *The Hindu Arabic numerals*, p. 135.

number of operations to *seven and no more* as does the *Carmen*, and its description of duplation as the adding of a number to itself, and its definitions of linear, surface and solid numbers, as well as several other points of resemblance suggest the *Algorismus vulgaris*, and have led me to the conclusion that the writer was a monk, with interests theological rather than mathematical, who was acquainted with both the works mentioned and must therefore have written later than 1200.

After the *Algorismus vulgaris* no new methods were introduced into the practical treatises on reckoning until the early 15th century when Prosdocimo de Beldamandi wrote his *Algorismus de integris*. In the introduction to this work, Beldamandi refers to the calculating slate and the custom of erasing figures in the course of an operation. He realizes that in such a process, it is difficult to find an error of calculation, and states that it is his intention to write a book in which this disadvantage will be eliminated.[1] Here we find addition, subtraction, mediation, duplation and multiplication explained exactly as they are taught today, though division and the extraction of square and cube root appear as in the older treatises. Frequent references are made to Boethius and Euclid, but that the work is founded upon that of Sacrobosco would be evident even without the acknowledgment made by the writer.

The algorisms of Jordanus Nemorarius and the *Algorithmus demonstratus* are treatises of a character quite different from those already mentioned. These presuppose a knowledge of the practice, and elaborate the theory of the arithmetical operations after the model of the *Elements* of Euclid. Beginning with definitions and axioms, a series of short propositions leads up to the general rule, but though interesting in their character, their influence upon the arithmetic of the middle ages is not in any way comparable with that of the practical treatises which I have mentioned.

[1] A facsimile of a page of Beldamandi's work is printed in Smith's *Rara Arithmetica*, p. 14.

To summarize briefly the results of this research, we may say that the elements of arithmetical calculation as taught today derived their definitions from the Greeks and from Boethius, and their methods from the Hindus; that the Arabic treatises have received too little appreciation, and were equaled only by those of the Hebrews of the same period; that the influence of the abacus, showing itself in expression and method is apparent in the Latin works, even when concerned wholly with the new reckoning; that the *Liber algorismi de pratica arismetrice*, based upon the arithmetic of Al-Khowarizmi, and other Arabic treatises was known and used by most of the later writers; and that up to the time of printing the *Carmen de Algorismo* of Alexander de Villa Dei, and the *Algorismus vulgaris* of Sacrobosco were the most widely read of all the Latin works.